PRACTICAL
FENG SHUI

SIMON BROWN

C CASSELL
ILLUSTRATED

To my father Michael John Hilton Brown

A WARD LOCK BOOK
This edition first published in the United Kingdom by
Cassell Illustrated
2-4 Heron Quays
London E14 4JP

First published 1997
02 20 19 18 17

Created and produced by
CARROLL & BROWN LIMITED
20 Lonsdale Road
London NW6 6RD

Publishing Director	Denis Kennedy
Art Director	Chrissie Lloyd
Project Editor	Sandy Carr
Assistant Editor	Steven Chong
Art Editor	Adelle Morris
Designer	Matthew Sanderman
Production	Christine Corton, Wendy Rogers
Commissioned photography	David Murray, Jules Selmes

British Library Catalogue-in-Publication Data
A catalogue record for this book is available from the British Library

ISBN 0--7063-7634- X

Printed and bound in Great Britain by The Bath Press

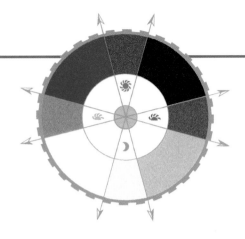

CONTENTS

FOREWORD

I first met Simon Brown in 1992, when he and his partner Dragana Sudzum interviewed me for a macrobiotic magazine. We had an instant rapport and I ended up interviewing them, since they were the experts. I

knew very little about healthy living, in fact. I had recently battled against a very public drug addiction and had lived on junk food for most of my life. Simon and Dragana became my "brown rice gurus". We built up a steady relationship and I now count them as two of my dearest friends.

I soon discovered that macrobiotics was more than brown rice and tofu. It was a complete way of life. Simon introduced me to the graceful art of Feng Shui, which he described perfectly as "a Shiatsu massage for your whole being". He said that certain areas of my home had the power to influence my life. It was a strange concept but one I found most intriguing.

Simon came to my home with his compass and set about redirecting my energies. This was achieved by repositioning the furniture, changing the lighting, and adding mirrors and beautiful plants. In my living room he found my relationship area, which quickly became home to a massive fig tree, a shimmering crystal and a gilt-framed mirror – such was my desire for better relationships.

Bringing in chi energy
Fresh flowers and clear water bring their own envigorating energies into the house. The bowl is refilled with fresh water every morning.

I hung one of my gold discs in the fame area and got rid of all the clutter in my hallway, further improving the flow of energy. My home certainly felt tidier and this alone had an amazing effect on my mental clarity. It helped me to focus on important parts of my life which had long been ignored. Watering my fig tree made me think of friends and lovers and relationships in general. Friends have since commented that my house is more inviting and it feels like a proper home. I can highly recommend Feng Shui.

Simon's book is a vibrant clear introduction to this ancient art, full of wonderful and simple ideas to make your life flow more generously. Enjoy!

BOY GEORGE

FENG SHUI TODAY

Feng Shui originated in China over 4000 years ago and its practice has a long history throughout the East. Similar ideas have also existed in other parts of the world at one time or another. The notion that the "spirit" or atmosphere of a place has an effect on your well-being is widely accepted, but in Feng Shui it has developed into a complex integrated system of theory and practice that embraces almost every aspect of people's lives.

> "Feng Shui" means "wind and water". It is the art of designing your home to promote success in life, health, wealth and happiness.

The underlying premise of Feng Shui is that everything in your surroundings, down to the smallest details of furnishing and decor, can either further your aims in life or work against you. By understanding the subtle currents of energy that flow through your body and through everything in the universe, you can arrange your living and working environments to help you reach your goals.

The key principles have developed over the centuries. The concept of yin and yang (pages 16–23) describes two broad types of energy which connect people and their surroundings. The Five Elements (pages 24–7) and the Eight Directions (pages 30–3) refine this further to provide a sophisticated set of principles for understanding the way energy moves through the home and immediate environment to affect all areas of life.

Applying these principles to your own life and circumstances can help you to get a job or understand why you have lost one. It can help you decide the best time to set out on a journey, embark on a new enterprise or a new relationship, and the most favourable direction to move. It can

POTENTIAL BENEFITS OF FENG SHUI

- Better sleep
- Selling a home
- Increased motivation
- Improved health
- Good start to a new career
- Growing business

- Getting a job
- Becoming pregnant
- More active sex life
- More harmonious family relationships
- Fame and respect
- Love and romance

- Being more assertive at work
- Better relaxation at home
- More stimulating social life
- Feeling more in control

help smooth difficult family relationships, or ease your way to finding a partner in life or business. It can make your work more productive and your leisure time more rewarding.

I have used Feng Shui extensively and the greatest benefit has been the feeling that I am more in control of my life. If something does not work out as I had hoped, I feel better able to understand why, and to come up with a new and more successful approach. Rather than you being the helpless victim of circumstance, it puts you in the driving seat. You can get the forces of nature to work with you rather than against you.

STYLES OF FENG SHUI

Feng Shui has been used in very different environments and cultures. It has been scrutinized by eminent philosophers and scholars as well as by Feng Shui masters. Not surprisingly, there have been changes in its long history, and different systems have developed. Some of these seem contradictory which can be confusing, so it is better to begin by studying one style rather than several simultaneously. Four styles are popular in the West: the Eight Directions or Compass Method, the Eight House Method, the Flying Star School, and the Form School or Black Hat Sect. The first

Natural kitchen
Food, which nourishes life, is prepared here, so kitchens are particularly important in Feng Shui terms. Natural wood surfaces and natural flame cookers such as Agas, are recommended (see pages 103–6).

three use a compass to assess energy flows through a building; the earth's magnetic field, solar energy and the planets are believed to be most influential. These systems are linked to an Oriental system of astrology known as Nine Ki. The Form School uses the surrounding mountains and entrance to a building as the basic orientation.

FOUR SCHOOLS

All four schools of Feng Shui share the basic principles of how energy moves, yin and yang, the Five Elements and Eight Trigrams. The differences relate to how they are applied.

The Compass Method is based on the idea that eight directions of the compass each experience a different kind of energy. A compass determines the directions in a home or room. The influence of specific features are assessed on the basis of their direction from the centre. Nine Ki astrology is used to understand the influence of the timing and direction of moving home and to determine the ideal time to make changes. The occupants' Nine Ki charts also have an effect.

In the Eight House Method the front of the house and its compass bearing determine the nature of eight segments or 'houses' within the

Cool bathroom
Plenty of light, fresh plants and flow-ers, tiled surfaces and the cool green and white decor help to avoid the unfavourable effects that bathrooms can have on the rest of the home (see pages 107–10).

Activating good energies
Ordinary elements of interior decoration and furnishing can be used to promote favourable Feng Shui. Mirrors, plants and candles are especially effective (see pages 119–53).

building. The occupants' Nine Ki charts determine the suitability of each segment for each individual, and, ideally, this will dictate where each person sleeps, works or spends the greater part of their time.

The Flying Star Method uses a compass bearing on the front of a building to orientate its own birth chart, determined by the construction date. The effect of the building's features and surroundings on the birth chart are assessed, and likely problems for the coming years anticipated.

The Form School originated in mountainous areas and uses the shape of the surrounding landscape and the building's entrance to determine the way energy flows through it. A grid of nine squares known as the Ba Gua provides information on how each area will affect the occupants.

I have practised the Form School and the Compass Method and have found the latter more satisfying for my particular style of Feng Shui, so the Compass Method and its accompanying Nine Ki astrology, as taught by Japanese masters, is the system used in this book.

APPROACHES TO FENG SHUI

When applying Feng Shui to your life there are several approaches. You may be planning to move to a new home or even to build a one, in which case you will have a bare canvas on which to work. More often you will already be settled in a home, but would like to improve the atmosphere there or to solve particular problems in your life. The problem-solving approach is often the most productive. It is better to focus on solving specific problems rather than to make blanket changes to your home. Make sure you do not use Feng Shui to invent problems that do not exist. If life is going well, limit the changes to fine-tuning. Implement one solution at a time and assess the result, before going on to another one.

Above all, do not expect Feng Shui to be the answer to all your problems. It is only one of many influences on your life. Your diet, your family background and general life experience, for example, all have profound effects. The success of Feng Shui depends largely on how realistic your expectations are. It is most effective when you can relate a problem to something about your home, and make the necessary changes.

The first step is to identify the problem. If you have been living in a place for some time assess how your life has changed since you moved in. When people move home their lives often change for better or worse. Make lists of areas where you have had problems, and those you would like to improve. Relationships, finances and career usually figure in either or both lists. Next work out more specifically why you are having these

Spacious dining room

Light, airy, uncluttered rooms are desirable for good Feng Shui. The round table seating eight is also ideal. The combination of pale colours, natural wood and fabrics is likely to produce a relaxed atmosphere for dining. The spiky plant adds its own revitalizing energy, but is placed well away from the table and will not direct cutting chi at the diners (see pages 87–92).

Relaxing living room

A favourable seating arrangement promotes family harmony and good conversation. Pastel colours and soft upholstery are soothing but there are also uplifting touches in the vertical striped fabric, tall plants and the mirror over the fireplace, which will reflect stimulating fire energy back into the room (see pages 79–86).

Harmonious furnishings

The shape of your furniture and the material it is made of will affect the balance of energies in a room. Soft materials such as wood, bamboo and wicker, and rounded shapes are calming. Hard shiny materials – ceramic tiles, glass, marble – and angular shapes are more stimulating (see pages 128–9).

problems. If you are in financial difficulties, for example, is it because your income has declined or your expenses have shot up? If you cannot find a romantic partner, is it because you do not go out and meet people, or overwhelm those you do meet? Is your career at a standstill because your efforts are not being noticed or you have lost your ambition?

The answers should suggest a solution: to make more money or cut down expenses, to be more sociable or less aggressive, to be more assertive, more motivated or set your horizons higher. Only now can you begin to think of applying Feng Shui to make sure your environment is helping you to achieve your aims rather than frustrating them.

FENG SHUI IN THE SOUTHERN HEMISPHERE

Various schools of Feng Shui have been practised in Australia and New Zealand for many years and there are different opinions as to how the principles should be adapted for the southern hemisphere. Some people feel north and south directions (see pages 30–3) should be reversed; others do not. Since the concept of yin and yang relates to the position of the sun, this must be reversed for the southern hemisphere – the sunny, more yang, side of buildings will be in the north, and the shady, more yin, side in the south. I suggest you concentrate initially on how the sun affects your building; reverse north and south directions but leave east and west in the same positions. Later, you can study more advanced planetary aspects of Feng Shui which could provide further insights.

HOW TO USE THE BOOK

CHAPTER 1 explains the basic principles of Feng Shui. It may be tempting to skip this and go straight to the practical applications but I strongly recommend that you make the effort to understand the basics first. Once you have grasped these you can design your own solutions to suit your tastes and the character of your home. Chapter 1 also provides an introduction to Nine Ki astrology which determines the best time and the most favourable directions for you to move home or make alterations to your present home. Finally, it describes the tools of Feng Shui and how to use them. You will need to arm yourself with these before reading further.

CHAPTER 2 explains the influence of the architecture of your home and of the landscape on the flows of energy there.

CHAPTER 3 provides advice on the location of each room in your home and recommendations for furnishing and decor.

CHAPTER 4 focusses on particular features of a home such as doors, windows and stairs as well as items of decor such as furniture, mirrors and plants..

Note: In artworks and compass diagrams the direction north is shown at the bottom, which is the traditional style on Oriental maps.

the PRINCIPLES of FENG SHUI

The concepts of chi energy, yin
and yang, the Five Elements and
the Eight Directions explain
how making changes to your
living space can transform your
life and fortunes; Nine Ki
astrology deals with the timing
of those changes.

chi energy

For thousands of years people have been aware of energy moving through the universe, connecting everything in it like a huge computer network.

What has come to be called 'chi' is a subtle flow of electromagnetic energy which links all things in the universe. Ancient peoples were probably able to sense its movement. Sites such as Stonehenge, Carnac and the Nazca lines, seem to have been constructed along so-called ley lines, believed to mark underlying concentrations of energy. They may have been built specifically to channel this energy: maybe their builders were in touch with the flow of energy and knew how to influence it.

In the Far East the understanding and control of energy flows underlies traditional healing systems such as acupuncture and Shiatsu as well as martial arts like Tai Chi, Qi Kong and Aikido. The energy has several names. In China it is called Chi, in Japan it is known as Ki (also spelt Qi) and in India Prana. There are no specific words for it in the West, although expressions such as 'atmosphere', 'mood', 'life-force' or 'spirit' describe how it is perceived. In this book it is referred to as chi energy. Chi is central to Oriental astrology and Feng Shui.

Chi stays mainly within entities such as human bodies, plants or buildings, but some of it constantly flows out and some flows in from other sources. Your own personal chi energy is always mixing with the chi energy around you. In this way you are connected to the immediate environment, and ultimately to the whole universe, as ripples of chi energy from far away reach you. Exceptionally sensitive people may be able to pick up advance information from these distant sources in the form of premonitions, visions or telepathy.

WIND AND WATER

The flow of chi energy from one entity to another is the basis of Feng Shui. The chi energy you take in from your environment influences your moods, emotions, physical energy and, over time, your health. Chi energy is carried through the environment by wind, water, the sun's solar energy, light and sound. It moves in a similar way to these natural phenomena except that, unlike some of them, it is able to flow through solid matter. It flows in and out of buildings mainly through the doors and windows, but some chi can enter and leave through the walls. It moves like water ebbing and flowing with the tides, and like air moving around the Earth. The name Feng Shui, which literally means "wind-water", reflects the way chi energy moves. The basic aim of Feng Shui is to enable you to position yourself where this natural flow of chi energy helps you to realise your goals and your dreams in life.

SUN

PLANETS

Heaven's force

Earth's force

Heaven's force

Earth's force

Earth's force

Earth's force

Earth's force

Heaven's force

MOON

Heavens's force and Earth's force
Chi energy radiating from the planets moves towards the Earth – Heaven's force. Earth radiates chi energy that moves away from it – Earth's force.

UNIVERSAL CHI

Chi energy flows not only throughout our planet, but through the entire solar system and galaxy. Our own planet, Earth, radiates chi energy that flows out and away from the planet. To the people who live on Earth this appears as chi energy moving upwards and is called Earth's force. At the same time, the planets surrounding Earth radiate chi energy which travels towards and into the Earth. This appears to us to move downwards and is known as Heaven's force. So the movement of chi energy on the surface of the Earth, and therefore in our homes and in our own bodies, is influenced by the Earth itself and the surrounding planets. As the position of the Earth, Sun and planets changes, so does the movement of chi energy, which in turn affects our own flow of chi energy. Feng Shui astrology (see pages 34–41) is the art of understanding these largescale movements of chi energy and predicting their effect on a particular person.

The spinning motion of the Earth means that more of Earth's force is thrown off at the Equator and less at the poles. Slightly more of Heaven's force will flow into the north and south poles. Earth's chi energy moves from the centre up through the Earth's crust, becoming more dispersed in some areas and more concentrated in others. These concentrations are thought to appear on the surface as ley lines.

As Heaven's chi energy reaches Earth its movement is altered by the landscape (hills, mountains, rivers), vegetation (trees, crops, grasses, bushes) and the ground itself (rocks, clay, soil, chalk). As Earth's force and Heaven's force mix across the surface of the planet various unique flows and eddies of chi energy develop. The same is true of buildings in a city. Low flat dwellings, skyscrapers, pointed roofs, domes and tree-lined avenues all determine how chi energy flows across the surface, and roads, rivers, railways, offices, factories, homes, entertainment centres, churches, graveyards and hospitals all have an influence on the nature of that energy.

CHI IN BUILDINGS

Buildings alter the flow of chi energy. Their shape, openings and the materials they are made of define the way chi energy flows through them (see Chapter 2). It moves most easily through doors and to a lesser extent through windows, so the orientation of a building to the sun and the planets will determine the kind of chi energy that enters it. This changes as the planets move through the sky, so there is a new pattern of chi energy each year, month, day and hour. The biggest changes occur each year (see pages 34–41). Features of the immediate surroundings, such as water or roads, further determine the kind of chi

CHI FROM THE PAST

Old buildings will have absorbed some of the chi energy linked with the happy or sad events that have taken place there. Most of this washes away with time, but a residue could stay for centuries.

Negative chi energy hangs on in parts of a building that are dark or damp, and can affect the lives of people living there. If generations of occupants have experienced similar misfortunes (for example, illness, divorce or bankruptcy), it could be caused by the Feng Shui of the building.

Before moving into a new home find out as much as you can about its history and that of the previous occupants. If there have been problems, you may be able to change the existing Feng Shui so that the chain of events is broken.

Fields of influence
The originators of Feng Shui sensed intuitively the influence of the electrical, magnetic and gravitational fields that pervade the universe.

DUST AND CLUTTER

Dust has its own chi energy, which tends to stagnate when it becomes stuck in one place. Clutter harbours old chi energy and makes it difficult for chi to move smoothly through a building. Stagnant and slow-moving chi deplete your vitality and make it difficult to look forward and be productive.

Clean your home regularly to revitalize its chi energy. Take rugs and bedding outside to air; empty and clean out cupboards, vacuum carpets thoroughly and wash or dry-clean curtains regularly.

At least once a year go through your possessions and put to one side the things you no longer use. Put them in storage, sell them or give them away.

energy that flows back and forth through the doors of the building. In an ideal situation chi energy flows harmoniously through the whole of a building. The design and interior decoration should enhance the kind of chi energy that furthers the aims and desires of the occupants and should exclude or minimize features that hinder them,

UNFAVOURABLE CHI ENERGIES

Some situations produce unhelpful types of chi, causing problems for a building's occupants, and even physical or mental ill-health.

NEGATIVE CHI Certain building or decorating materials have a negative effect on chi energy: synthetic fibres, synthetic building materials, artificial lighting and air conditioning all add their own artificial chi energy, which negatively influences the chi energy of the occupants, and could lead to mental and physical exhaustion.

STAGNANT CHI Slow-moving and stagnant chi energy is produced by dark corners, cluttered rooms and dampness. They can lead to a slowing down of your own chi energy, which may cause serious health problems and a loss of direction in your life.

FAST-FLOWING CHI Chi energy moving quickly in a straight line can destabilize the flow through an entire building, so long corridors, straight paths or several features in a straight line should be avoided. Fast-moving chi energy directed towards you could push away some of your own chi energy, making you feel insecure and under attack. (See also Cutting Chi, below.)

cutting chi

If chi energy passes a sharp corner it begins to spin and swirl, forming eddies and whirlpools like a fast-flowing stream passing a sharp bend. This is called cutting chi and can occur inside or outside buildings. It can make your own chi energy swirl, leading to disorientation and confusion and, in time, ill-health. There are various remedies (see pages 62 and 85).

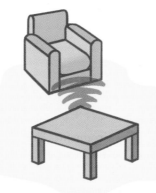

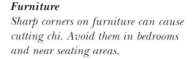

Furniture
Sharp corners on furniture can cause cutting chi. Avoid them in bedrooms and near seating areas.

Neighbouring buildings
If the corner of a building points at your home, it can cause cutting chi. Plant bushes to shield the front door.

PERSONAL CHI

To appreciate how chi energy in the environment influences you, it is necessary to understand how it moves within your own body. It flows through it in much the same way as blood. Along the centre of the body are seven concentrations of energy called chakras (see right), which are similar to large organs where blood concentrates. Spreading out from the chakras are 14 paths of chi energy known as meridians. These flow along your arms, legs, torso and head. Like blood vessels and capillaries, they take chi energy to smaller and smaller channels until each cell is nourished by both blood and chi energy.

While blood carries oxygen and nutrients, chi energy carries thoughts, ideas, emotions and your dreams in life. It also carries some of the chi energy from the environment. Therefore, what you think and where you think it, will have a direct influence on the cells in your body. The influence of the mind on physical health is well-established. Many people have experienced the benefits of positive thinking and some claim to have used it to recover from serious illness. Similarly, people have been healed by moving to a new location. Travelling to spa towns or locations with special healing properties has a long tradition.

Chi energy operates as a two-way process whereby the way you think influences your chi energy, and your chi energy influences the way you think; so your environment will influence your chi energy and that change will alter the way you think and feel. Like trees planted in the best soil for their needs, we thrive if we are planted in the best chi energy. By moving from one building to another, one city to another, or one country to another, you have the opportunity to change your own chi energy and therefore the way you think and feel. If the chi energy of the place where you live matches the chi energy you require for happiness, then it will have a very positive influence on your life. Unfortunately, it is also possible that your home may work against you, and the chi energy of some places could negatively affect your well-being.

Many factors affect the chi energy that comes into your body – among these are food, weather and the people you are with. In Feng Shui terms, the primary influence is the chi energy of the environment. This includes your home, your place of work and the surrounding landscape. A building itself has an influence. Being in a large ornate building such as a museum or cathedral can be inspiring, exciting and stimulating, whereas a small cosy place such as a cottage, café or bar is more relaxing and intimate. A building's location also helps shape the kind of chi that enters your body. The chi energy in rural areas is different from that in a city, and travelling to other parts of the world also gives you the chance to experience very different kinds of chi energy.

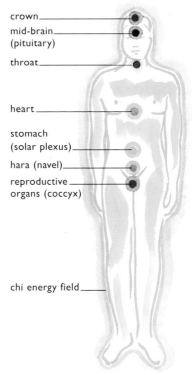

crown
mid-brain (pituitary)
throat
heart
stomach (solar plexus)
hara (navel)
reproductive organs (coccyx)

chi energy field

The chakras
Chi flows through the human body by means of channels called meridians which act rather like blood vessels. They radiate from seven key points in the body where energy concentrates, called chakras. Typically, chi extends at least 10cm and up to 1 metre outside your skin.

yin and yang

Everything in the world can be seen in terms of two kinds of energy: passive and active, or yin and yang, which is one of the fundamental principles of Feng Shui.

The concept of yin and yang offers a comprehensive way of looking at the world and how it affects you. It makes it possible to adjust your relationship with people and your surroundings so that you can place yourself in favourable rather than unfavourable situations. Ultimately, you will be able to use your knowledge of yin and yang to get more out of your life with less effort.

At the time of a full moon, for example, people become more yang, which means they are more active, want to go out more and are generally more sociable. Conversely, at the time of a new moon they become more yin – more peaceful, spiritual, relaxed and inward-looking. So if you want to organize a party, the days before or during the full moon are the best times. People will be more outgoing and more in the mood for a get-together. At the new moon you risk fewer people turning up and those who do will be quieter.

Similar principles can be applied to your home, diet, exercise, work and leisure activities. They all have aspects that are more yin or more yang, and you can encourage them to work for you or against you depending on your needs at the time.

basic principles

EVERYTHING IS EITHER MORE YIN OR MORE YANG

Yin and yang are relative terms used to compare everything in the universe. Things are more yin or more yang depending on what they are compared with. For example, resting is more yin than working, but more yang than sleeping. Yin and yang can describe physical things or non-physical things. You need to be clear about how the terms are applied in particular cases. For example, a flame is more yang than a stone in terms of a process: the flame produces heat and light. But the structure of stone is more yang than flame: more solid, compact and harder.

EVERYTHING SEEKS A STATE OF BALANCE

Although everything is either more yin or more yang, as an entity it seeks some kind of balance. Individually nothing is in perfect balance, nor can it be as everything is either more yin or more yang. Something that is more yin can reach a more balanced state with something that is more yang. Often we drift either side of the middle path. For a while we become more yin and then make changes that make us more yang, and vice versa.

GLOBAL YIN AND YANG

The position of the sun and moon, and the seasons make you feel more yin or yang, and you instinctively adjust your lifestyle to keep a balance.

DAY AND NIGHT   During the morning the sun rises in the sky making people feel more yang until it reaches its highest point at midday. As the sun begins to descend, you become more yin; at midnight, the sun reaches its most yin point. If you have difficulty getting things done, morning, when you feel more active and yang, is the best time to concentrate your efforts. After midday, you'll feel more like relaxing when the more yin chi energy will be on your side.

PHASES OF THE MOON   In the few days leading to the full moon you become progressively more yang. This is a helpful time to be more active, but you could also be accident prone. After the full moon and during the days leading to the new moon you become gradually more yin. This is the time to cultivate inner peace.

SEASONS   Autumn and winter are cold and damp, both yin qualities. You feel the need for warming foods like hot porridge, thick soups and hearty stews which are more yang and help create a balance in the body. Conversely, in spring and summer the air becomes warmer and drier, a more yang atmosphere. More yin foods such as fresh fruits, raw vegetable salads and drinks are cooling.

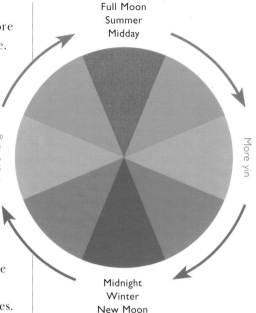

Full Moon
Summer
Midday

More Yang

More yin

Midnight
Winter
New Moon

Yin and yang in time
The environment is most yang at midday, in high summer and at full moon. It is most yin at midnight, in midwinter and at the new moon.

YIN AND YANG ATTRACT EACH OTHER

Things that are more yin attract other things that are more yang, rather like the poles of a magnet. As you become more yin you attract things that are more yang into your life and vice versa. A simple example is that by eating something more yang, such as dry salty snacks, you begin to crave liquids, which are more yin. An extreme of yin or yang will attract its extreme opposite. For example, someone who becomes very yang – angry, aggressive or violent – may attract the opposite – a stay in hospital or prison (because of an accident or crime).

NOTHING IS WHOLLY YIN OR WHOLLY YANG

Everything has some yin and some yang. Nothing is entirely one thing or the other, though everything will be more one thing or another. It is better to think of yin and yang in terms of varying shades of grey, rather than black and white. Even the most ruthless criminal will have a tender spot just as the gentlest person will have known frustration and anger. There is always something positive in a negative situation just as there is something negative in a positive situation.

EVERYTHING CHANGES

The relationships between things that are more yin and things that are more yang are constantly changing. Everything is always moving from being more yang to being more yin or more yin to more yang. For example a person might be more yang – irritable, frustrated and pushy – but in the process of becoming more yin – relaxed, peaceful and calm. In the long term the direction you are going is more important than where you are now.

Yin landscapes
A gently undulating rural landscape is more yin, and conducive to a slow peaceful way of life.

Yang cities
A bustling city full of stimulation and excitement is more yang and supports a dynamic active way of life.

YIN AND YANG IN THE LANDSCAPE

Landscapes and cityscapes have a yin and yang dimension. Generally, peaceful locations -- for example, woodland close to a slow-moving river or shaded green meadows – have a more yin influence on chi energy. This kind of location would be helpful if you have retired and feel you want to lead a quieter life. Busy cities are more yang and better for people who want a busier life. The active fast-moving chi energy there will support and help you if you are, for example, trying to build up your career or start a business.

Locations that are exposed to the sun are also more yang. The sunny sides of a mountain or valley, or an apartment or office block are all more yang. Shady locations are more yin and will help you develop the more reflective parts of your life. Locations that have no exposure to sunlight are not recommended for living in.

The vertical aspects of things are more yin, so the top of a landscape has a strong yin quality.

MOUNTAINS, SEA AND CITIES

Traditionally, people go to the mountains to meditate. The atmosphere in such places is more inward and more conducive to developing inner feelings and thoughts. Mountains are also more charged by Heaven's force (see page 13), which is helpful for spiritual matters. This type of chi energy originates from the more yin heavens. At the same time there is a downward movement towards the centre of the earth, which means it is becoming more yang.

The sea is also a more yin environment and is supportive to rest, relaxation and internal healing. The chi energy here is Earth's force (see page 13) which rises from the centre of the earth and is stronger at sea level. Although it originates from a more yang source, its upward movement means it is in the process of becoming more yin.

Interestingly, great spiritual revelations have come from people going to the mountains to meditate -- consider the prophets in some of the world's main religions, and the Buddhist orders in Nepal and Tibet, whereas great practical realisations, for example Feng Shui and Oriental astrology, have come from meditating or contemplation on the banks of a river closer to sea level.

Flat landscapes are comparatively yang. The chi energy here supports busier more active lifestyles and this is typically where large human settlements such as towns and cities, with their connecting road links, have developed. Heaven's force and Earth's force are more evenly balanced here and the energy is well suited to the generation of new ideas and being able to put them into practice.

YIN AND YANG IN THE HOME

The sun's movement through the sky alters the flow of chi energy through your home. As the sun rises through the sky from morning to midday, the east, south-east and south of your home will become energized by more yang chi energy. In the southern hemisphere this will be the east, north-east and north of your home. After midday as the sun descends in the sky, the west, north-west and north of your home are energized by more yin chi energy. In the southern hemisphere this will be the west, south-west and south.

To check these directions, take a compass and stand in the centre of your home. Move around until you have a consistent compass reading. The needle of your compass will be pointing north. Alternatively, watch the sun move through the sky. Wait until it reaches the highest point. If you are in the northern hemisphere the sun is now south of your home; in the southern hemisphere it will be to the north.

The sunny side of your home is better for activities that require you to be more yang. The shady side is better for those that require you to be more yin. If you are already too yin or too yang, spend more time in a place that has the opposite type of chi energy in order to become more balanced. For example, if you get angry quickly and have difficulty relaxing you could be too yang and should spend more time in the yin side of your home. If you move your bedroom to a yin part of the building you will be taking in more peaceful yin chi energy as you sleep.

On the other hand, if you feel tired, depressed and tearful you could be too yin. Work or do things in the sunny side of your home to take in more yang chi energy. The effect of yin and yang on the different parts of your home will also influence how you allocate the various rooms there (see pages 70–1).

BUILDING SHAPES

The chi energy of a building is also affected by its overall type and shape. For example, tall thin vertical buildings like the classic skyscraper have more yin chi energy, whereas short wide buildings are more yang. The chi energy at the top of a tall building will have slightly more Heaven's force and sunlight will be a stronger factor, and the bottom slightly more Earth's force, so that being at the top of such a building can be stimulating for having big ideas, and being on the ground is better for making those ideas a reality.

Looking at a building from above, if it is long and narrow it is more yin, if it is round, octagonal or square it is more yang. The more compact the shape the more yang the building. A house or apartment that spreads out in many directions will tend to have more yin chi energy.

Yin and yang shapes
Tall thin and long narrow buildings are more yin, low squat buildings in compact shapes such as squares, circles and octagons are more yang.

Yin and yang food
Eating the right food can help balance personal yin and yang. The foods above range from the most yang (salt, meat) at the top to the most yin (liquids, sugars) at the bottom.

PERSONAL YIN AND YANG

People can be more yin or more yang. More yin people tend to be relaxed, physically supple, sensitive, creative and imaginative. However, if they are too yin, they can be lethargic, slow and prone to depression. Conversely, more yang people tend to be alert, quick, more active, and more able to concentrate and pay attention to detail. If they are too yang they can become tense and irritable, angry or physically stiff and tight.

With an understanding of yin and yang you can adjust these natural tendencies to your advantage. It is possible to tailor your diet (macrobiotics is specially designed for this) and lifestyle to improve your performance or overcome a health problem. If you find it difficult to concentrate, for example, and your work is adversely affected, decide first if you are too yin or too yang. Concentration is a more yang activity, so a lack of it suggests you are too yin. The solution would be to avoid more yin foods such as alcohol, sugar and coffee, and include some mineral-rich yang foods, such as root vegetables, fish and natural soya sauce.

ARE YOU TOO YIN OR TOO YANG?

One way to assess this is to compare yourself to other people. When you are too yin, other people will seem more aggressive, irritable and impatient with you. They will want you to hurry, while you want to relax and take things easy. When you are too yang, you will find other people slow, indecisive and quiet. You may find yourself becoming irritable and angry with them. Some people are always more yin than most people, some are always more yang, and others will be more in the middle.

If there is an imbalance in your life, the first step is to decide whether you are too yin or too yang. Look at the chart of personal yin and yang features opposite and make a judgement. Of course, everyone has a mixture of yin and yang characteristics, and it is not always easy to make a judgement one way or the other. Another approach is to focus on the changes you are trying to make to your life. If you find it difficult to relax, for example, you are likely to be too yang; if are are frequently listless and depressed, you are probably too yin.

The next step is to look at the chart of yin and yang influences opposite. This lists food, exercise and activities in terms of yin and yang. If you are more yin, look for more yang foods, exercise and activities to introduce into your life. If you are more yang, look for more yin influences to become involved with.

PERSONAL YIN AND YANG FEATURES

MORE YANG BODY TYPES

Broad
Short
Short fingers and toes
Eyes close together
Thin lips
Round head
Small eyes
Balanced proportions
Less body hair
Big eyes
Full lips
Long fingers and toes
Tall
Thin

MORE YIN BODY TYPES

MORE YANG EMOTIONS

Angry
Frustrated
Irritable
Competitive
Ambitious
Enthusiastic
Confident
Relaxed
Peaceful
Gentle
Sensitive
Tearful
Insecure
Depressed

MORE YIN EMOTIONS

MORE YANG MENTAL QUALITIES

Quick thinking
Detailed
Precise
Logical
Ordered
Creative
Flexible mind
Broad-minded
Imaginative
Slower

MORE YIN MENTAL QUALITIES

MORE YANG PHYSICAL QUALITIES

Tight gaunt skin
Stiff
Strong
Fast
Quick reactions
Flexible
Supple
Loose
Soft
Slow
Tired
Listless
Weak

MORE YIN PHYSICAL QUALITIES

YIN AND YANG INFLUENCES

MORE YANG FOOD

Salt
Meat
Eggs
Fish
Grains
Root vegetables
Beans
Leafy vegetables
Tofu
Salads
Fruits
Liquids
Ice cream
Sugar

MORE YIN FOOD

MORE YANG EXERCISE

Boxing
Karate
Football
Tennis
Aerobics
Running
Fast walking
Slow walking
Relaxed swimming
Stretching
Tai Chi
Yoga
Meditation

MORE YIN EXERCISE

MORE YANG PHYSICAL ACTIVITIES

Skiing
Surfing
Horse riding
Sailing
Dancing
Gardening
Walking in the
country
Massage
Sunbathing
Resting
Sleeping

MORE YIN PHYSICAL ACTIVITIES

MORE YANG MENTAL ACTIVITIES

Financial accounts
Studying
Playing chess
Computer
programming
Playing cards
Painting
Chatting
Listening to music
Reading
Watching television

MORE YIN MENTAL ACTIVITIES

NOTE The lists are arranged so that the most yang examples appear at the top, and the most yin at the bottom.

using yin and yang in your home

The shapes, materials and colours of objects you put in your home make the chi energy there more yin or more yang. This provides you with ways to alter the chi energy of your home to suit your needs.

Fast food restaurants are a good example of how this is done very effectively. The colours are often red, orange or yellow; the surfaces hard and shiny; the layout angular and ordered. This makes for a more yang environment which attracts people into the restaurant, but once they are there the atmosphere is not relaxing and they leave as soon as they finish eating.

Contrast this with a typical bedroom. Carpets, curtains and bed clothes provide soft yin surfaces. Popular colour choices are greens, blues and pastels – more yin colours and shades. All this makes for a soothing ambience which is ideal for sleeping.

MORE YANG SHAPES

Circular
Octagonal
Square
Broad rectangle
Broad oval
Long thin rectangle
Thin and wavy

MORE YIN SHAPES

MORE YANG COLOURS

Red
Orange
Yellow
Green
Blue

MORE YIN COLOURS

SHAPES

Rounded shapes are generally considered to be more yin than straight-sided shapes – a long thin curved table is more yin than a rectangular table. A circle is an exception to this because, although it is rounded, it is also the most compact shape and is therefore more yang. Objects that are compact with straight or angular lines are also more yang in shape.

COLOURS

These have a great influence on yin and yang by reflecting different frequencies of light back into the room. People react to colours in a very personal way, but in general red, orange and bright yellow make us feel more yang, greens and blues more yin. Pastel shades of any colour are more yin than stronger brighter shades of that colour. The larger the area covered by a particular colour the greater its influence will be. Even small touches of strong bright colours, such as scarlet or purple, however, can be effective. A painting which includes a patch of brilliant red can change the chi energy of an entire room.

MATERIALS

What things are made of – especially the material and finish of their surfaces – encourages either a quicker more yang flow of chi energy or a slower more yin flow. Generally, hard, shiny, reflective surfaces such as glass, polished marble or stainless steel speed up the flow of chi energy whereas soft, matt or textured surfaces such as natural wood and fabric slow it down.

Yin and yang objects
Colour can make things more yin (blues, greens) or more yang (reds, oranges, yellows).

MORE YANG
MATERIALS

Glass
Marble
Granite
Polished stone
Unpolished stone
Shiny metal
Dull metal
Polished hardwoods
Natural hardwoods
Polished softwoods
Natural softwoods
Wicker
Fabric

MORE YIN
MATERIALS

MORE YANG
FLOORS

Marble
Stone
Hardwoods
Softwoods
Cork tiles
Rush matting
Rugs
Carpets

MORE YIN
FLOORS

MORE YANG WINDOW
TREATMENTS

Shutters
Metal slatted blinds
Wooden slatted blinds
Paper blinds
Cloth blinds
Curtains
Light curtains
Full draped curtains

MORE YIN WINDOW
TREATMENTS

MORE YANG
FURNISHINGS

Stone sculptures
Mirrors
Glazed paintings
Metal furniture
Hardwood furniture
Softwood furniture
Paper screens
Upholstered furniture
Tapestries
Large cushions

MORE YIN
FURNISHINGS

five elements

The concept of the Five Elements is a refinement of the principle of yin and yang. Instead of two types of chi energy, there are five: tree, fire, soil, metal and water.

The Five Elements are most often applied in Oriental medicine but they also relate to the home and environment. Like yin and yang, the Five Elements are linked with seasons and times of day. The year is divided into five seasons, rather than four, with an extra season appearing between summer and autumn, called early autumn or late summer.

Each of the Five Elements describes a certain kind of chi energy and these can be related to a particular direction based on the way the sun moves around the sky during the day and over the year. The different types of chi energy are best appreciated by imagining that you are outside in nature at the appropriate time of day and year (see opposite)

THE FIVE ELEMENTS IN YOUR HOME

The Five Elements are associated with five directions, which are related to the movement of the sun through the day. In the morning the east of your home soaks up the upward chi energy known as tree. As the day progresses, the sun moves from east to south and charges up the south of your home with radiating fire chi energy. Later, the sun begins to go down and brings more settled soil chi energy into the south-west and centre of your home. As the sun sets, the west of your home will take in inward-moving metal chi energy. During the night, the north of your home benefits from flowing water chi energy.

Five-Element chi energies are taken into your home most intensively at the relevant times of day and remain there until recharged again the following day. So the east of your home, for example, will always be charged to some extent with tree energy regardless of the time of day.

The Five Elements are also found in your home in their pure form. Tree energy is there in the form of wood, paper and tall plants; fire in the form of stoves, fireplaces and lighting; soil in the form of china, clay and plaster; metal in the form of iron, silver, stainless steel and other metals; water in the form of ponds, sinks, bathrooms and aquariums.

SHAPES, COLOURS AND MATERIALS

The Five Elements are associated with shapes, colours and materials (see chart on page 26), and can be introduced into your home in these forms, applied to the building itself and its interior decoration.

Wallpaper with vertical stripes, for example, will bring more uplifting tree chi energy, making the ceiling appear higher and the room more spacious. A star print will increase fire chi energy, creating an exciting atmosphere. Horizontal or check patterns enhance soil energy, which makes the room feel cosier. Round shapes boost metal energy, making it feel more complete and finished. Wavy or irregular patterns add water chi energy, conveying a peaceful flowing atmosphere.

Appropriate colours can be applied to walls, ceilings and floors or furnishings. Strong colours like red and black will be effective even when they cover a relatively small surface area. A vase of red flowers could be enough. Similarly, what your furniture is made of – wood or metal, for example – will have an influence.

These effects will be especially intense if you combine colours with particular patterns or materials. For example, green wallpaper with vertical stripes would represent tree energy and so on. This ability to manipulate the existing chi energy using the Five Elements is the basis of many Feng Shui remedies.

five-element chi energies

Tree
You are walking down a tree-lined path in the early morning in spring as the sun breaks the horizon. The overriding feeling is of energy moving up, like the branches of a tree reaching up into the sky. The tree is coming into leaf, everything is looking forward to a new day and a new year.

Fire
It is the middle of a hot summer's day. Nature is in full bloom. The tree is in full leaf. Bright light and colourful flowers fill the picture. The energy seems to expand in every direction, radiating like the heat of a glowing fire.

Soil
Think of an afternoon in early autumn. The leaves have changed colour and are beginning to fall . The sun is getting lower in the sky. The overall feeling is of energy moving down into the ground.

Metal
It is evening in late autumn and there is a beautiful sunset. As the red sun sinks below the horizon the feeling is of energy gathering in, and nature storing up its energy ready for the winter. Energy is moving inwards and becoming solid, which mirrors the process by which metal is formed.

Water
Finally it is a damp, frosty night in midwinter. On the surface all is quiet and still, but powerful changes are taking place in the soil below and there are strong currents of water beneath the ice. Water is calm on the surface but flowing beneath. This type of chi moves in a similar way.

FIVE ELEMENT	SHAPES	COLOURS	MATERIALS	MEANING
TREE East/South-east 	rectangular tall thin vertical	green	wood wicker rush bamboo paper	life growth vitality activity
FIRE South 	pointed star serrated triangular pyramid diamond zigzag	red	(plastic is the material associated with fire chi energy, but is not recommended for use in the home because of its negative effects on chi energy – see also page 129)	passion warmth excitement expression
SOIL South-west/Centre/ North-east 	squat low flat wide check horizontal	yellow brown	plaster china clay ceramics bricks natural fibres (e.g. cotton, linen, wool, silk) softer stone (e.g. limestone)	comfort security steadiness caution
METAL West/North-west 	round domed arched oval circular spherical	white gold silver	stainless steel brass silver bronze copper iron gold harder stone (e.g. marble, granite)	richness solidity leadership organization
WATER North 	irregular curved chaotic wavy amorphous	black	glass	depth power flexibility tranquillity

FIVE-ELEMENT RELATIONSHIPS

Two flows of chi energy govern the relationships between the Five Elements: the support cycle and the destructive cycle (right). These can be compared to the annual agricultural cycle. Remember that each of the Five Elements relates to a particular season: water to winter, tree to spring, fire to summer, soil to early autumn, metal to late autumn.

WATER In winter we prepare the ground and plant the seeds. If spring is fine, they will grow. But if there are late frosts, they will destroy the new shoots, and there will be nothing to show in summer. Water supports tree, but if tree is deficient, water destroys fire. Think of water feeding a tree, but extinguishing fire.

TREE If spring goes well, the fields will be full of crops in summer. But if summer is poor, due to lack of sun or heavy rains, the crops will rot in the ground in the early autumn. Tree supports fire, as wood is fuel but, if fire is deficient, tree destroys soil.

FIRE After a good summer the crops will ripen in early autumn. But if the weather is cold and cloudy in early autumn, the crops will not ripen to be ready for the late autumn harvest. Fire supports soil just as ash enriches the earth but, if soil is deficient, fire can destroy metal.

SOIL With plenty of sun in early autumn there will be a good harvest in the late autumn. But early frosts or heavy rain in late autumn will destroy the harvest and there will be no new seed to plant in the winter. Soil supports metal just as minerals in the soil form metal ores, but if metal is deficient, soil will destroy water.

METAL If the crop has set seed in the late autumn and conditions in winter are good, the seed can be planted for the following spring. But harsh winter conditions may destroy the seed before it can to sprout. Metal supports water, but if water is deficient metal will destroy tree.

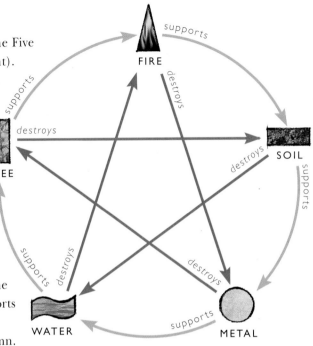

Cycles of support and destruction

In the support cycle (orange) chi energy moves in a circle clockwise from one Five-Element position to the next, changing itself into the next element. Each element supports the next, but the supportive activity is draining, so each element is drained by the following one – water supports tree, but is also drained by tree. This means the support cycle can be used to calm chi as well as boost it.

In the destructive cycle (red) chi moves in straight lines from one element bypassing the second element and going straight to the third. It does this if the second one is deficient in some way, but the effect of the first element on the third one is destructive. The destructive cycle can be used positively in Feng Shui, but generally the main objective is to build up deficient energy.

These relationships are summarized in the chart (left).

5 ELEMENT	SUPPORTS	DESTROYS	DRAINS
WATER	tree	fire (if tree is weak)	metal
TREE	fire	soil (if fire is weak)	water
FIRE	soil	metal (if soil is weak)	tree
SOIL	metal	water (if metal is weak)	fire
METAL	water	tree (if water is weak)	soil

USING THE FIVE ELEMENTS

The Five Elements and the relationships between them (see page 27) provide a model for understanding the universe and the interaction of the different types of chi energy. They can be used to manipulate the flow of chi energy in your home and are the basis of many Feng Shui remedies and solutions. Using your knowledge of the supportive and destructive cycles, and depending on what you are trying to achieve or what problem you are trying to solve, you can enhance one type of Five Element chi energy, calm another or maintain a balance. This manipulation is carried out by introducing objects associated with the relevant elements (see below) into the appropriate space.

Suppose, for example, you have a room in the south of your home, and you wish to increase the chi energy there. The south is linked with Five-Element fire chi energy. Fire is supported by tree energy. So you can boost the chi energy of the south by building up fire energy itself or

introducing five-element objects

Five-Element chi energies can be introduced into a space in pure form – actual plants, fire, soil, metal or water – or in the form of representative objects. The most powerful objects are those which combine the shape, colour and material of an element (round, silver, metal balls for metal energy, or a low, brown, terracotta trough filled with brown earth for soil energy, for example).

Other colour schemes linked to compass directions (see pages 30–3) can also be used: for instance, red in the west for metal and purple in the south for fire.

Water
Use clean fresh water itself, glass objects or things that are black or irregular in shape. Those above include glass dishes and pebbles, black wavy stems and fabric.

Tree
Use actual plants, wood or paper and tall, thin green objects. Those above include a green pot, a tall green vase, tall lamp with paper shade and green frame.

by adding supportive tree energy. Fire energy is linked with pointed shapes, the colour red, lights and fire itself, so to boost it introduce candles, red star-patterned wallpaper and bright lights into the room.

Tree chi energy is linked with tall thin rectangular shapes, the colour green and materials wood and paper. Trees and tall plants are the element itself, so tall plants, green vertical-striped wallpaper, wooden floors and a paper screen would all increase tree chi energy in the room.

To reduce the chi energy in a southern room you would need to bolster the Five-Element chi energy that is draining to fire, namely soil. Low clay sculptures, the colour yellow, and low spreading plants growing in plenty of soil would bring more soil chi energy into the room.

The support cycle can be used to calm chi energy as well as build it up. To calm chi energy in the north, for example, you could grow trees or tall plants because they represent Five-Element tree energy, which drains the water energy of the north.

Fire
Use fire itself and red or pointed objects. Those above include an oil lamp, star-shaped candle holders, a red star, red flowers in a red vase and red fabric.

Soil
Use soil or clay itself and yellow/brown or low rectangular objects. Those above include a clay trough, yellow flowers, a square plate, frame and checked fabric.

Metal
Use metal itself and round, silver, gold or white objects. Those above include a round metal frame, a round metal pot, a round wire tray and silvery balls.

eight directions

The principle of the Eight Directions takes yin and yang and the Five Elements a step further. This concept identifies eight different kinds of chi energy.

THE CHI OF THE CENTRE
▼

There is a ninth type of chi energy – that of the centre. This energy holds the greatest power and therefore implies greater possibilities but also greater risks than the Eight Directions. It is changeable and has two extremes: productive and destructive. It is linked with the Five Element soil, the number 5 and the colour yellow but, unlike the Eight Directions, has no links with a trigram, symbol, family member, time or season.

In terms of arranging your home, it is best to keep the centre of your home and of each room as empty as possible

---

The eight directions of the compass are each associated with a different kind of chi energy. Each direction is also linked with a trigram from the *I Ching* (see below), a Five Element, a symbol of the natural world, a family member, a Nine Ki number, a colour, a time of day and a season. Together these produce a detailed picture of the type of chi energy found in that direction. The centre also holds its own characteristic energy, which is very powerful (below left).

TRIGRAMS The author of an ancient Chinese philosophical text called the *I Ching* devised the trigrams, which each consist of three broken or solid lines (representing yin and yang) on top of one another symbolizing a particular combination of energies. For example, the trigram for water is a solid line with broken lines above and below: outwardly flexible and quiet (yin) but with deep strength inside (yang).

FIVE ELEMENTS Each direction and the centre is linked to at least one of the Five Elements (see pages 24–9). The north and south each have their own Five Element, the other directions all share a Five Element.

SYMBOLS Where two directions share a Five Element, they each have a different symbol. For example, the east and south-east share Five Element tree, so they each have a different symbol: thunder in the east and wind in the south-east.

FAMILY MEMBERS Each direction is linked with a family member, adding another layer of meaning to the picture. These are based on a traditional Oriental family, which may seem inappropriate nowadays, but can be interpreted symbolically in whatever way is most meaningful.

NINE KI NUMBER These are the numbers in Japanese Nine Ki astrology (see pages 34–41) that refer to the individual characteristics of people determined by their date of birth. Each direction and the centre has a Nine Ki number associated with it.

COLOUR Each direction and the centre has a colour associated with it. They are also based on Japanese Nine Ki numbers. The colours of the east, south-east and centre are the same as those linked with the Five Elements; the rest are different.

TIME OF DAY This is determined by the time when the sun is in the relevant direction. The chi energy there is strongest at that time, so the chi energy in the south of your home is strongest at midday.

SEASON Each direction is linked with a season and this is when the chi energy there will be strongest: so the chi energy in the south of your home is strongest in midsummer.

the eight types of chi energy

A distinctive type of energy is found in different sectors of a home, a room or a landscape. These sectors are defined by their direction from the centre of the home, room or landscape, which is determined by an ordinary compass (see pages 42–6). A room in the north of your home, for example, will carry the chi energy of the north; but different parts of that room will also hold some elements of the chi energies of the other directions. Eight Directions chi energies encompass both yin and yang and the Five Elements as well as the other associations defined opposite. The diagram below summarizes the general picture; the chart overleaf describes the implications for each type of chi energy in detail.

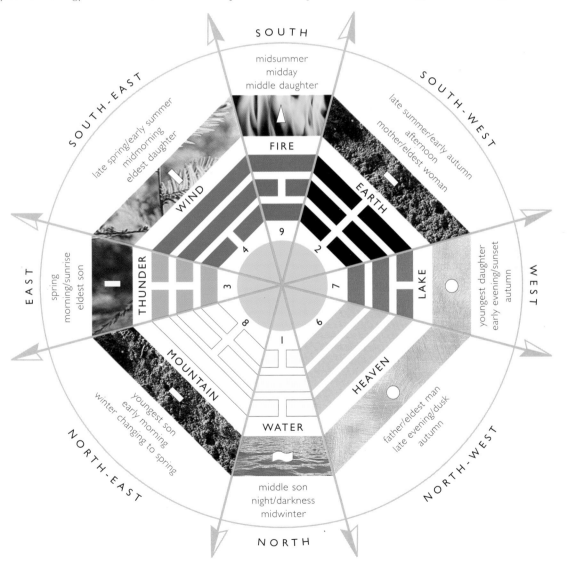

SOUTH
midsummer
midday
middle daughter

SOUTH-EAST
late spring/early summer
midmorning
eldest daughter

SOUTH-WEST
late summer/early autumn
afternoon
mother/eldest woman

EAST
spring
morning/sunrise
eldest son

WEST
youngest daughter
early evening/sunset
autumn

NORTH-EAST
youngest son
early morning
winter changing to spring

NORTH-WEST
father/eldest man
late evening/dusk
autumn

NORTH
middle son
night/darkness
midwinter

FIRE
WIND
EARTH
THUNDER
LAKE
MOUNTAIN
HEAVEN
WATER

9 4 2 3 7 8 6 1

DIRECTION	CHI ENERGY

NORTH

		Trigram	yin/yang/yin
		Five Element	water
		Symbol	water

Family member middle son
Nine Ki number 1
Colour off-white
Time of day night/darkness
Season midwinter

North represents conception — life beginning — when the child begins to develop its individual characteristics in its mother's womb, almost independent of the world. On the surface all seems quiet, but inside powerful changes are taking place. The chi energy is quiet, most active at night and in midwinter. It relates to sex, spirituality and isolation.

The yin lines of the trigram provide flexibility and a superficially passive nature. The yang line represents power and strength deep down. Water chi energy also implies depth and movement with flexibility. It can change direction easily, but this is done in a less disruptive way than with other types of chi energy. Traditionally, the middle son symbolizes affection, but with a great independent spirit. Off-white has an almost translucent quality most easily produced with a gloss finish.

NORTH-EAST

		Trigram	yang/yin/yin
		Five Element	soil
		Symbol	mountain

Family member youngest son
Nine Ki number 8
Colour brilliant white
Time of day early morning
Season winter changing to spring

This is when the child learns to interact with the world. It develops individuality, competitiveness directed at survival and preparing for the next phase, and strength and stubbornness. The north-east is part of a north-east/south-west axis where both directions and the centre have the same Five Element — soil. Energy can move very quickly because it does not have to transform itself into another element — making these directions unstable. North-east chi is strong piercing and quick to change direction. It is most active just before dawn and towards the end of winter.

The trigram represents strength and activity over stillness. The mountain symbolizes a rocky harshness. Youngest sons are traditionally spoilt and competitive which adds motivating, sharp, direct qualities. Brilliant white also creates a bright, sharp atmosphere.

EAST

		Trigram	yin/yin/yang
		Five Element	tree
		Symbol	thunder

Family member eldest son
Nine Ki number 3
Colour green
Time morning/sunrise
Season spring

In this phase the child is ready to embark on a career. It is a time of ambition and new beginnings. The chi energy is active and focussed — and most intense at sunrise.

The trigram has a solid yang line beneath two broken yin lines, allowing the yang energy to move forcefully up through the yin lines before retreating to a more tranquil state. The tree provides an upward thrusting energy, and the image of sunrise adds the idea that it is the beginning of a new day. Thunder provides great power, aggression and the urge to go out and make things happen. The eldest son traditionally takes on the job of providing for the family after the parents retire; he is the family's future and this chi energy is linked with ambition, putting ideas into practice and realising dreams. The green of the east is bright, stimulating feelings of growth, freshness and vitality.

SOUTH-EAST

		Trigram	yang/yang/yin
		Five Element	tree
		Symbol	wind

Family member eldest daughter
Nine Ki number 4
Colour dark green/blue
Time of day mid-morning
Season late spring/early summer

This is the phase of maturity and harmonious progress, when long-term relationships are formed including engagements and marriage. The chi energy here is busy and active, but less sharp than that of the east. It is strongest in mid-morning and early summer when the sun is rising in the sky.

The trigram has a yin line sitting beneath two yang lines. Gentleness at the heart is protected by great activity on the surface. The symbol of wind brings persistence and power to this chi energy, but is less aggressive and dramatic than thunder. The eldest daughter is gentler than the eldest son and the chi energy here encourages orderly harmonious progress. Dark green is deeper and steadier than the bright green of the east, symbolizing growth and vitality but of a more mature kind. Some blues have similar qualities.

DIRECTION	CHI ENERGY

SOUTH

Trigram yang/yin/yang
Five Element fire
Symbol fire
Family member middle daughter
Nine Ki number 9
Colour purple
Time of day midday
Season midsummer

This phase represents the prime of life when hard work has paid off and the benefits of success and public recognition can at last be enjoyed. The chi energy of the south is fiery, passionate and brilliant, and is most active at midday and in midsummer when the sun is at its highest point. If the chi energy in this part of a home is moving well, fame and social success could be the result.

The trigram is a yin line sandwiched between two yang lines. The chi energy is active and dynamic on the surface, but flexible and flowing on the inside. The middle daughter brings her outgoing, extrovert and sociable nature to this direction. It is also linked with intelligence and beauty. The colour of the south is purple – particularly the shade that is found at the base of a flame. It instils passion, excitement and heat.

SOUTH-WEST

Trigram yin/yin/yin
Five Element soil
Symbol earth
Family member mother/eldest woman
Nine Ki number 2
Colour black
Time of day afternoon
Season late summer/early autumn

This chi energy is symbolized by the more settled state of middle age – the time for spending more time at home – and family harmony is the dominant theme. The south-west is on the same unstable axis as the north-east, but the changes are less sudden and disruptive. The chi energy here is more settled and slow, and is most active in the afternoon and late summer as the sun sinks in the sky. The atmosphere is conducive to consolidation and methodical progress, creating a more cautious environment

The trigram has three yin lines, implying a more receptive, yielding, female energy. The symbol of the mother, also brings femaleness and encourages family harmony. Similarly, the earth carries the idea of supporting and nourishing life. Black, like the colour of rich, dark soil, enhances the atmosphere of nurturing and supportiveness.

WEST

Trigram yin/yang/yang
Five element metal
Symbol lake
Family member youngest daughter
Nine Ki number 7
Colour red
Time of day early evening/sunset
Season autumn

This is the time of late middle age, approaching retirement. It is time to let go, relax and enjoy the fruits of your labours. The chi energy of the west is linked with financial income and the harvest, and is most active at sunset and in autumn.

The trigram has a yin line over two yang lines. The calm of the surface is supported by strength below, which creates a playful movement of chi energy. The symbol of the lake brings a deeper, more reflective quality, and metal energy, according to some schools of Feng Shui, is linked with money. The youngest daughter reinforces the playful nature of this direction, and is also associated with the pursuit of pleasure. The colour of the west is red, like the fiery glow of a brilliant sunset. It enhances feelings of romance, joyousness, style and contentment.

NORTH-WEST

Trigram yang/yang/yang
Five Element metal
Symbol heaven
Family member father/eldest man
Nine Ki number 6
Colour silver white
Time of day late evening/dusk
Season late autumn/winter

This is the final phase in the cycle of life – old age. By this time the accumulation of experience has led to wisdom, and the possibility of helping others through the earlier stages. The chi energy of the north-west is linked with leadership, organization and planning ahead, and is most active at dusk and in late autumn or winter.

The three yang lines of the trigram bring a powerful, male chi energy. The symbol of heaven adds dignity, wisdom and an image of superiority. The father brings ideas of respect, authority and responsibility. This is a particularly significant direction for the father, eldest man or main wage-earner of either sex in the family. The association of silvery white with the hair of an elderly person reinforces the impression of dignity, pride and wisdom.

nine ki astrology

The Compass Method of Feng Shui is concerned with time as well as space. Not only can you find out how to arrange the space in your home, but also the best time to do it.

There are favourable and unfavourable times to do things. If it is advantageous to move your bed to a certain position, there will also be an advantageous time to do this. What you do and when you do it should both work in your favour, whether you are implementing Feng Shui recommendations or moving to a new home.

People's lives often change radically after moving home, and one of the biggest influences can be the timing and direction of the move. This is not surprising when you think of what happens in the natural world. When you move a growing plant from one place to another, you first take it out of its existing soil, then you have to move it without damaging it, and replant it in the most suitable soil and at the right time of year for it to flourish in its new environment.

It is much the same with people. Wherever you live your chi energy mixes with that of your local environment. When you leave that place it is as though you literally tear your roots out of the soil. The direction and timing of your move determine how well your personal chi energy can mix with chi energy of the new place. If the new chi energy is favourable, you have the chance to flourish. If not, you could face problems. But as well as carrying risks, moving to a new home can also be an invaluable opportunity to enhance your life and boost your chances of health, wealth and happiness, just as a weak and listless plant will miraculously revive when transplanted to more suitable soil.

THE MAGIC SQUARE

Timing a move to be compatible with the forces of nature can make all the difference between success and failure. You should no more leave it to chance than you would embark on an ocean-going voyage without map, nautical instruments or weather charts.

The Magic Square (see left) functions as both a map and timetable to chart the movements of chi energy for each year, month, day and hour. Feng Shui practitioners use it to work out the ideal time and direction to move to a new home, the best time to undertake major renovations and the most favourable dates to implement Feng Shui recommendations. It is also used to find the best day and direction to travel to an important event, to sign a contract or start a new business.

Fu Hsi is said to have discovered the Magic Square when he saw a turtle – a sacred animal in China – climb out of the River Lo, and was struck by the pattern of water droplets on its shell. In a moment of deep

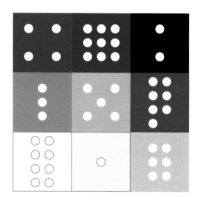

Fu Hsi's discovery
This pattern of numbers, known as the Magic Square, forms the basis of Nine Ki astrology and Feng Shui. It was discovered thousands of years ago by the Chinese Emperor Fu Hsi, legendary originator of China's great philosophical text the I Ching, *or* Book of Changes.

meditation he came to believe that this could explain the movement of energy through the universe. The droplets were arranged in the nine compartments of the turtle's shell with a group of 5 in the centre and the remaining groups between 1 and 9 around it so that they added up to 15 in every direction. In Feng Shui these numbers represent nine types of chi energy, and are described in detail on pages 30–3.

NINE KI

Nine Ki is the name for Feng Shui astrology in Japan. Nine refers to the nine numbers in the Magic Square; Ki is the Japanese word for chi energy. The arrangement of numbers in the Magic Square with 5 in the centre is the standard Nine Ki chart, and represents the prevailing pattern of energies in certain years. Each year the pattern changes and this is represented by a different Nine Ki chart.

There are nine possible year charts (see right) which repeat over a cycle of nine years. As each new year begins a new number takes up the central position and the other numbers are rearranged around (only in the standard chart do they add up to 15 in each direction). Each year the central number decreases by 1, so for 1997 the central number is 3, in 1998 it is 2 and so on.

From this you can discover the Nine Ki number (the central number) of your birth year (see page 37). This is also your personal Nine Ki number. It represents the type of chi energy prevalent in the year you were born, which imprints you for life in much the same way as a fingerprint or configuration of DNA. It affects how you relate to other types of chi energy, whether of people or places, and helps determine the conditions which are supportive or destructive to your well-being and aims in life. A proper Nine Ki chart is based on the year, month and day you were born, but this complex calculation is best undertaken by an experienced practitioner of Nine Ki astrology. Here we use year charts only.

NINE KI ASSOCIATIONS

FIVE ELEMENTS This relationship is based on the position of the Nine Ki numbers in the standard chart (right). For example, in the standard chart, 1 is in the north, which represents Five Element water. People with the Nine Ki number 1 will have features of Five Element water in their character, so they could be incompatible with Nine Ki 9 because of its link with Five Element fire. People tend to be more comfortable when their Nine Ki number is in a position whose Five Element energy is compatible with theirs. If your Nine Ki number is 1, for example, you will feel happier in years when 1 is in a tree (e.g. 1997, 1998) or metal (e.g. 2001, 2010) position since water harmonizes with tree and metal.

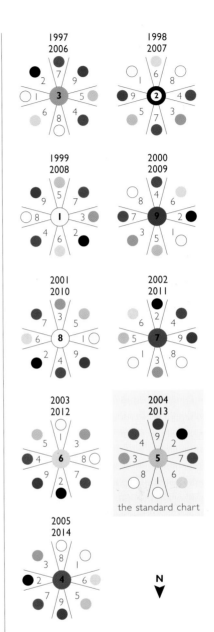

Nine Ki year charts
There are nine possible year charts, representing nine patterns of chi energy. The changing position of your Nine Ki number will give you clues about the influences on you in a particular year. For example, if your number is 5 the chi energy of your birth year is soil (centre) but in 1999 you will take on some of the characteristics of fire, because 5 is in the fire position (south) that year.

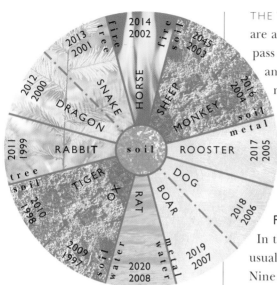

Influential associations
Nine Ki links with the Five Elements and the animals of the year are especially important for timing moves and making changes to your home (pages 38–41).

YOUR NINE KI NUMBER
▼

With your Nine Ki number you can discover:
• the type of chi energy present in your birth year giving you insight into your character, needs and aspirations.
• the type of chi energy present each year, and the position of your own chi energy in that chart.
• the most favourable directions for you to move in any year.
• the best time to make changes to your home.

THE TWELVE ANIMALS The 12 symbolic animals of Chinese astrology, are associated with particular compass directions (in this case the compass is divided into 12 rather than 8 directions). Each year one of the animals becomes more active. The cycle of change moves clockwise round the compass and begins again every 12 years. In 1998, for example, the Tiger (east-north-east) becomes active, followed in 1999 by the Rabbit (east) and so on. Consequently, there will be a special concentration of energy in the east-north-east in 1998, and in the east in 1999. This has particular implications for timing a move to a new home.

FINDING YOUR PERSONAL NINE KI NUMBER

In the Western calendar the year starts on 1 January, but in Nine Ki it usually it begins on the 3, 4 or 5 February. The chart opposite shows the Nine Ki numbers for the years 1910–2017, including the exact date and time (Greenwich Mean Time or GMT) each year begins.

Use it to look up your Nine Ki number. If you were born in January 1950, for example, your Nine Ki number is 6 – the number for 1949; if you were born in March 1950 it would be 5. If you were born close to 3, 4 or 5 February in any year, you will need to take account of the difference between the GMT shown on the chart and your local time. New York is five hours behind GMT, for example, so the year changes in New York five hours earlier than GMT – the time shown on the chart. In 1958 the year began on 4 February at 14:57 GMT, so in New York it would have begun at 14:57 minus 5, or 09:57 local time.

The same applies when calculating dates for moving. If you plan to move home on the 4 February 1998 before 08:01 GMT, you use the chart for 1997. In New York the equivalent time would be 4 February 1998 before 03:01 local time.

The colours on the chart are Eight Directions colours (see page 31) and are related to the position of the numbers on the standard chart. They are auspicious colours for those with the associated Nine Ki number: green is auspicious for anyone with Nine Ki number 3, for example.

The symbols on the chart represent the type of chi energy associated with that number: wind, thunder, heaven and so on (see pages 32–3).

It is possible to calculate the Nine Ki Year Number for women using a different method whereby each year increases by 1 instead of decreasing by 1. The numbers for men and women are the same when their Nine Ki Year Number is 3; so, for example, 1952 is 3 for men and women and 1953 and 1954 would be 4 and 5 for women instead of 2 and 1. In this book I use the system whereby men and women born in the same year share the same Nine Ki Year Number.

NINE KI NUMBER	9	8	7	6	5	4	3	2	1
COLOUR									
SYMBOL	fire	mountain	lake	heaven		wind	thunder	earth	water
5 ELEMENT	fire	soil	metal	metal	soil	tree	tree	soil	water
Year / Beginning date / Time (GMT)	1910 4 Feb 23:41	1911 5 Feb 05:33	1912 5 Feb 11:11	1913 4 Feb 17:01	1914 4 Feb 22:53	1915 5 Feb 04:34	1916 5 Feb 10:31	1917 4 Feb 16:18	1918 4 Feb 22:06
	1919 5 Feb 04:00	1920 5 Feb 09:43	1921 5 Feb 15:34	1922 4 Feb 21:28	1923 5 Feb 03:13	1924 5 Feb 09:06	1925 4 Feb 14:58	1926 4 Feb 20:49	1927 5 Feb 02:46
	1928 5 Feb 08:31	1929 4 Feb 14:19	1930 4 Feb 20:11	1931 5 Feb 01:53	1932 5 Feb 07:42	1933 4 Feb 13:28	1934 4 Feb 19:13	1935 5 Feb 01:03	1936 5 Feb 06:47
	1937 4 Feb 12:36	1938 4 Feb 18:32	1939 5 Feb 00:20	1940 5 Feb 06:15	1941 4 Feb 12:07	1942 4 Feb 17:57	1943 4 Feb 23:51	1944 5 Feb 05:39	1945 5 Feb 11:26
	1946 4 Feb 17:18	1947 4 Feb 23:03	1948 5 Feb 04:50	1949 4 Feb 10:40	1950 4 Feb 16:29	1951 4 Feb 22:29	1952 5 Feb 04:07	1953 4 Feb 09:52	1954 4 Feb 15:42
	1955 4 Feb 21:29	1956 5 Feb 03:15	1957 4 Feb 09:07	1958 4 Feb 14:57	1959 4 Feb 20:47	1960 5 Feb 02:38	1961 4 Feb 08:29	1962 4 Feb 14:24	1963 4 Feb 20:17
	1964 5 Feb 02:08	1965 4 Feb 07:57	1966 4 Feb 13:46	1967 4 Feb 19:32	1968 5 Feb 01:19	1969 4 Feb 07:04	1970 4 Feb 12:50	1971 4 Feb 18:37	1972 5 Feb 00:23
	1973 4 Feb 06:13	1974 4 Feb 12:08	1975 4 Feb 17:56	1976 4 Feb 23:48	1977 4 Feb 05:38	1978 4 Feb 11:28	1979 4 Feb 17:21	1980 4 Feb 23:10	1981 4 Feb 04:59
	1982 4 Feb 10:53	1983 4 Feb 16:38	1984 4 Feb 22:27	1985 4 Feb 04:18	1986 4 Feb 10:05	1987 4 Feb 15:57	1988 4 Feb 21:42	1989 4 Feb 05:28	1990 4 Feb 09:20
	1991 4 Feb 15:04	1992 4 Feb 20:51	1993 4 Feb 02:42	1994 4 Feb 08:27	1995 4 Feb 14:18	1996 4 Feb 20:10	1997 4 Feb 02:00	1998 4 Feb 08:01	1999 4 Feb 13:51
	2000 4 Feb 19:39	2001 4 Feb 01:35	2002 4 Feb 07:20	2003 4 Feb 13:08	2004 4 Feb 18:57	2005 4 Feb 00:38	2006 4 Feb 06:31	2007 4 Feb 12:16	2008 4 Feb 17:59
	2009 3 Feb 23:55	2010 4 Feb 05:40	2011 4 Feb 11:31	2012 4 Feb 17:28	2013 3 Feb 23:05	2014 4 Feb 05:05	2015 4 Feb 10:55	2016 4 Feb 16:40	2017 3 Feb 22:37

To find a favourable year for an important event, consult the chart below, then check the position of your Nine Ki number in the Nine Ki years charts (page 35). For example, a good year for starting a family would be one where your Nine Ki number is in the water (north) position or the earth (south-west) position.

EVENT	FAVOURABLE POSITION
Getting married or starting new relationships	Wind/south-east Lake/west Earth/south-west
Starting a new business or new career	Thunder/east Wind/south-east Fire/south Lake/west Heaven/north-west
Winning prizes and competitions	Mountain/north-east
Starting a family	Water/north Earth/south-west
Retirement	Lake/west Heaven/north-west

NINE KI TIMING

Each year the movement of chi energy changes to a new pattern and influences your own chi energy in a different way. If your Nine Ki number is 1, for example, you were born with the characteristics of water chi energy, but in 1998 you move into the position of wind chi energy (south-east) and take on some of its characteristics. By looking at the chi energy of the coming years it is possible to plan ahead using the ambient chi energy to help you achieve your aims.

To put this into practice, find your own Nine Ki year number and the Nine Ki number of the year you are interested in (see page 37). Then locate your number on the Nine Ki chart for that year (that is, the chart with the year's Nine Ki number in the centre, see page 35). The position of your Nine Ki number on the year chart determines the influences on your life during the year in question. Suppose your Nine Ki number is 7, and you are interested in the influences on your life in 1998. The 1998 year number is 2, and 7 is in the water (north) position in the 2 chart, so if you look at the chart opposite you will see that 1998 could be a quiet year for you, though if you want to have a baby it would be a good year to conceive. It is a good year, too, for relaxation and study, though there could be a risk of health problems or financial difficulties.

Another approach is to find favourable years for important life events, in which case consult the Life Events chart (left).

MOVING HOME

Each year your personal chi mixes best with chi energies found in one or more of the Eight Directions. Since the pattern of chi changes from year to year, the directions that are favourable to you change. When you move home the timing and direction of the move determine your compatibility with the chi of the new place, with profound consequences for your life in general. By examining the Nine Ki chart of the year of your move, you can predict the changes which may lie in store for you.

First take a map which includes your home area and the areas you are considering moving to, and mark your current home on it. Draw a line from your home going due north. Then draw or trace the Eight Directions on the map so that the centre is over your home and north is aligned with north on your map (see pages 46). This will show you the arrangement of the Eight Directions from your home. The next step is to eliminate potentially harmful directions (see chart on page 40).

Having eliminated the unfavourable moves, a number of directions will remain as possible options. Each one carries a different influence. Consult the chart opposite to establish which influences are likely to be most helpful to you, given your situation and your aims in life.

POSITION OF YOUR NINE KI NUMBER	PREVAILING INFLUENCES FOR THE YEAR	RISKS
THUNDER (east)	A good year for being active, making a new start, in a new business or a new Job. Favours ambition, work, gaining promotion and putting ideas into practice. Particularly favourable for Nine Ki numbers 3, 4 and 9. If your Nine Ki number is 1, let opportunities come to you rather than initiating your own projects.	Rushing decisions, overworking and becoming frustrated.
WIND (south-east)	A good year for harmonious progress, starting a new business or new job. Favours creativity, communication and getting married especially if your partner is also in a favourable position. Particularly favourable for Nine Ki 1, 4 and 9. If your Nine Ki number is 3, you may be seeking relationships, but find harmony difficult to achieve.	Being too persistent, not taking advice.
CENTRE	A changeable year, not a good time for initiating anything new. Ride the changes rather than trying to impose your will on events. Ideas and plans originating in this year may well be changed in the following year. Defer major decisions if possible. Less unfavourable for Nine Ki numbers 2, 5, 6, 7, 8 and 9.	
HEAVEN (north-west)	A good year for organization, leadership and for planning ahead. Managers could find their position strengthened. Favourable for intuition and self-knowledge. Particularly favourable for Nine Ki numbers 1, 2, 5, 6 and 8. If your Nine Ki number is 7, you may have problems communicating your intentions and making progress.	Becoming arrogant, self-righteous and overbearing.
LAKE (west)	A good year for contentment, for romance, pleasure and enhancing your income. Favourable for starting a new relationship or getting married, for retirement and selling a business. Particularly favourable for Nine Ki numbers 1, 2, 5, 6, 7 and 8. If your Nine Ki number is 9, you might encounter problems with finances or romance.	Lack of motivation, and overspending in the pursuit of pleasure.
MOUNTAIN (north-east)	A good year for motivation and competitiveness, for achieving your ambitions through hard work. Think carefully before making decisions and be more cautious than usual. Particularly favourable for Nine Ki numbers 5, 6, 7, 8 and 9. If your Nine Ki number is 2, proceed slowly this year especially where family matters are concerned.	Rushing things in your determination to succeed.
FIRE (south)	A good year for being sociable and passionate. Favours attracting attention and gaining fame or pubic recognition. Particularly favourable for Nine Ki 2, 3, 5, 8 and 9. If your Nine Ki number is 4, resist tendencies to separation.	Being argumentative and provoking rifts with people.
WATER (north)	A quiet year, good for relaxation and studying. Favourable for women to conceive and, in general, for self-health programmes and increased vitality including sexual vitality. Particularly favourable for Nine Ki numbers 1, 3, 4 and 7. If your Nine Ki number is 6, do your best to stay out of the public eye, and guard against sexual scandals.	The dramatic contrast with last year may cause health or financial problems.
EARTH (south-west)	A good year for steady progress and consolidating gains. Favours friendships, for enhancing family harmony, home-building and making the most of what you have. A good year for giving birth. Particularly favourable for Nine Ki 2, 5, 6, 7 and 9. If your Nine Ki number is 8, you may find it difficult to motivate yourself.	Over-cautiousness, timidity, becoming dependent on others.

NOTE The sequence of the directions in the chart reflects the movement of your Nine Ki number over the years. Reading the influences in the chart in order, you will see how the influences affecting you are likely to change from year to year.

favourable and unfavourable moves

The criteria which make the direction of a move to a new home unfavourable are listed below. The charts show the results for the years 1997–2011. To discover favourable directions, find the chart for the year you intend to move. Your Nine Ki colour (see page 37) is shown in favourable directions for you. If your colour is off-white, for example, in 1997 moving south or north-east would be favourable; in 1998 moving north or south would be. Each year some directions are unfavourable for everyone.

UNHELPFUL DIRECTIONS

TOWARDS 5 This takes you towards the most powerful chi, which can be productive or destructive. Your health, career or business could be destroyed.

AWAY FROM 5 You would be moving away from great power and your chi could be weakened, risking accidents and robberies.

TOWARDS YOUR NINE KI NUMBER This is like trying to force the same poles of magnets together. Poor health, stress and tension could result.

AWAY FROM YOUR NINE KI NUMBER You would travel away from your own chi. You risk low confidence, feeling empty, and inability to organize your life.

AWAY FROM THE ANIMAL OF THE YEAR You would move into a deficiency of energy, risking family separation, the break-up of relationships or contracts.

TOWARDS AN INCOMPATIBLE FIVE ELEMENT If the Five Element chi there destroys yours it could be harmful and cause turbulence and upheaval.

TOWARDS A NUMBER OPPOSITE ITS USUAL POSITION This can cause unpredictability and unforeseen problems.

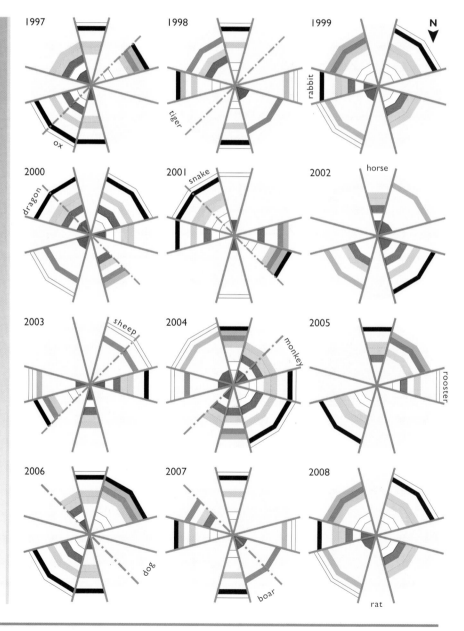

MAKING CHANGES TO YOUR HOME

The principles are essentially the same as finding the best time to move. The aim is to alter the flow of chi energy in a part of your home at a time that will be advantageous for you. This applies to major building works, and renovations. Using special Feng Shui calendars with detailed information on months and days, it is possible to calculate exact dates that are favourable for making changes, even relatively small changes like painting a room or installing an aquarium. Here, however, we are concerned only with the changes between years, which will be relevant for any large-scale changes you intend making to your home such as adding an extension, conservatory or swimming pool, or extensive redecoration.

The first step is to draw up an accurate floor plan of your home, find the centre and transfer a chart of the Eight Directions or superimpose a transparency of the Eight Directions as shown on pages 42–6. Next find the Nine Ki year chart for the year when you hope to make the changes (page 35) and ascertain the active animal of the year (see page 36). Transfer the number 5, your own Nine Ki number and the active animal to their appropriate directions for that year. The diagram on the right shows an example of this for a Nine Ki 9 person in 1999.

PROBLEM SECTORS

In the following list, the first two areas cause the greatest problems.

THE POSITION OF 5   Avoid changing your home in this segment of the floor plan. It could result in serious problems or hold-ups with the project itself, particularly if it includes major building work or renovations. In the long term it could make your lives more stressful, unpredictable and changeable.

OPPOSITE 5   Changes in this part of the home could lead to accidents. In the long term you could feel weaker and more vulnerable.

IN AND OPPOSITE YOUR NINE KI NUMBERS   Locate your own number and those of other members of your household. Where the family is large, consider mainly the parents or principal wage-earners, or anyone who is experiencing special problems. Changes in these sectors can upset the home, leading to particular stress and loss of confidence for the individuals involved.

OPPOSITE THE ACTIVE ANIMAL   Either leave this area alone or build up the chi energy in this part of your home. Plants and lights would have this effect. Adding something more yang in terms of colour, shape or material would be beneficial (page 22–3). Alternatively, use Five Element solutions (page 26–7). Add something that has the colour, shape and material of the Five Elements associated with this position and the preceding one.

SOLUTIONS
▼

If your last move was towards or away from 5 or your Nine Ki Year Number, you can reorientate your chi energy more favourably.
• Move temporarily in a helpful direction, sleep there for three months, then return home in a favourable direction. If you move to another continent, staying two months at your destination would be enough. On your return sleep every night at home for the first two or three months.
• Travel all the way around the world in a positive direction. On your return sleep in your home every night for two months.
• Make the first journey of the day to a destination in a helpful direction, for example to a café or a park. Spend about 20 minutes there.

1999

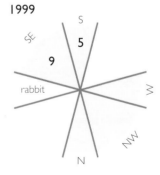

Making changes to your home
In 1999 a person with Nine Ki number 9, for example, should avoid major changes in the south (position of 5), north (opposite 5), south-east (their Nine Ki number), north-west (opposite their number) and west (opposite the animal of the year).

tools of feng shui

A few simple devices which you can make yourself will enable you to put the principles of Feng Shui into practice in your own home.

To apply the principles of Feng Shui to your home you first need to assess the pattern of chi energies there. This involves finding out which parts of your home fall in which directions, and therefore which parts are characterized by the different types of chi energy. In order to do this you must have a detailed accurate floor plan of your home on which to align a grid of the Eight Directions. If one is already available, make sure all details relevant to Feng Shui considerations are marked on it (see right). If not you will need to draw one up yourself.

"Your home" in this context refers to the space you own, rent or occupy. It could be a house or apartment. If it is an apartment, the plan should cover only those areas of the building that are yours, for your sole use. Later, you can assess the apartment within the whole building.

equipment

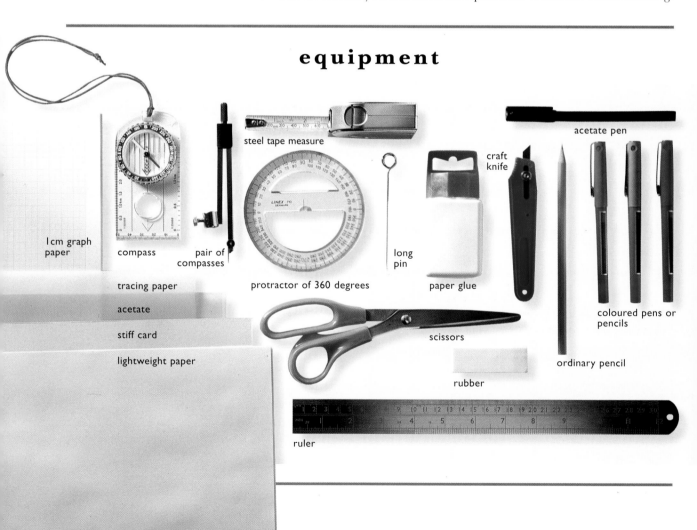

1cm graph paper

compass

pair of compasses

steel tape measure

protractor of 360 degrees

long pin

paper glue

craft knife

acetate pen

coloured pens or pencils

tracing paper

acetate

stiff card

lightweight paper

scissors

rubber

ordinary pencil

ruler

THE FENG SHUI FLOOR PLAN

If your home has more than one floor, make a separate plan for each one. Draw them accurately and to scale, using graph paper to make the job easier (see below). Include on the plan all the internal walls, all doors, windows, staircases, fireplaces. Also mark any likely problem features (see pages 76–7), such as protruding corners, sloping roofs or overhead beams, and fixed features that are important in Feng Shui terms, namely, fireplaces, sinks, fixed cookers, baths, showers, lavatories and so on. Finally, indicate the likely positions of significant movable items such as beds, desks, chairs, sofas and dining tables.

The next step is to find the centre of your home (see page 44) and of all the main rooms (especially where they are used for more than one function such as kitchen/dining rooms).

Finally, you need to align the plan with the grid of the Eight Directions (see pages 45–6). This will enable you to assess the balance of chi energies in your home at a glance.

drawing a floor plan

MEASURING THE ROOMS

Using a long retractable steel measure, note the length and width of each floor of your home, then of each room, and of staircases and corridors. Measure into alcoves and bay windows if appropriate.

Convert the measurements to a convenient scale, for example 1 metre = 1 cm. So if your room measures 5.2 x 3.5 metres, the rectangle on the plan would have to measure 5.2 x 3.5 cm.

Transfer the measurements to the plan in the appropriate positions. Add to the plan in scale all windows, doors and fitted store cupboards, wardrobes and kitchen units. Indicate on the plan the way the doors open into the rooms.

Adding relevant features
Mark on the plan all details relevant in Feng Shui terms (see above). Mark the fixed features in one colour, the movable ones in another, and the problem features in a third colour.

finding the centre

To determine the directions on your floor plan, first find the centre of each floor and of each of the main rooms. The easiest shapes to handle are simple squares and rectangles. Irregular shapes are rather more complicated. There is a mathematical method for finding the centre of irregular shapes, but the easiest way is to find the balancing point of the shape using a long pin.

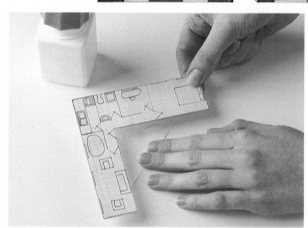

Finding the centre of squares and rectangles
Draw lines between opposing corners. The centre of the shape is the point where they intersect.

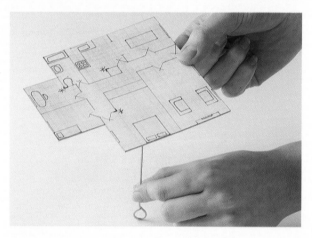

Finding the centre of irregular shapes
Photocopy or trace the shape of the floor or room, transfer or paste it on to stiff card and cut it out. Hold the card horizontally and try balancing it on the point of a long pin. Move the pin until you find the balancing point. This is the centre of the shape. Transfer it to the floor plan.

Finding the centre of L-shapes
If you cannot find the balancing point of an L-shape, the centre may be outside the shape. Glue a piece of lightweight paper over the area between the wings of the building where the centre is likely to be. This gives you something to balance on the pin, but light enough not to affect the centring of the shape.

aligning the grid of the eight directions

The grid of the Eight Directions is shown on page 46. It includes a marker for magnetic north. Copy the grid on to transparent film or tracing paper, or draw it on using a protractor and pair of compasses,

and cut it out roughly. Next align the grid with the floor plan using a compass. Some styles of Feng Shui use a complex compass called a Lo Pan. In this style an ordinary compass is sufficient.

GETTING A CONSISTENT COMPASS READING

Many objects distort compass readings: things made of iron or steel, electrical appliances, concealed metal beams, water tanks, water or gas pipes. Walk around your home holding the compass steady until the reading is consistent in several parts of a room. Use this room to find north on your plan.

Finding magnetic north on the floor plan (right)
Place the plan on a flat surface so that the walls on the plan align with the same walls in the area you are in. Place the compass on the plan so that its centre is over that of the plan. Turn the compass so the needle lines up with the marker line. Mark the plan at this point and draw a line to the centre.

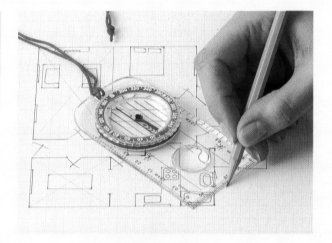

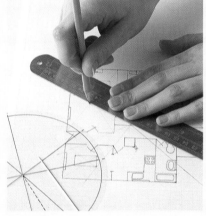

Use the same methods to assess the directions in each of the main rooms.

Aligning the grid of the eight directions
Place the transparent grid over the floor plan aligning the centres on both. Push a pin through the centres. Rotate the grid until the line pointing north on the grid aligns with magnetic north on the floor plan.

Transferring the directions
You can now read off the directions in your home through the transparent grid. Alternatively, with a pencil mark off the points around the grid on your floor plan. Draw lines between those points and the centre.

the grid of the eight directions

The grid below is used to determine the directions, and therefore the pattern of chi energy in a home (see pages 44–5). Different Feng Shui schools draw up the grid in different ways. Some divide it into eight segments of 45 degrees, others into four segments of 30 degrees and four of 60 degrees, which synchronizes the Eight Directions with the 12 animals of Chinese astrology. This is the system I use.

Note: In artworks and diagrams the direction north is shown at the bottom rather than the top, which is the traditional style on Oriental maps.

your HOME and its SURROUNDINGS

The architecture of the building
itself and certain features of the
landscape around it have
profound effects on the pattern
of chi energies in your home,
and this can affect many aspects
of your life favourably or
unfavourably.

the structure and shape of your home

The physical nature of your home determines the way chi energy flows through it and thus how the energy will affect you. The longer you stay in a home with a particular shape the more it can influence your life.

When you spend a good deal of time in a particular building you become aware of the relationship between its shape and structure, and its atmosphere. A long narrow building, for example, feels quite different from a square one. Such differences are in part the result of differences in the flow of chi energy, which can be affected by a number of factors: the materials used in the construction of the building, whether it has extensions or indentations, the balance or imbalance of the eight types of chi energy, and its exposure to sunlight.

Even the basic shape can be significant to Feng Shui analysts. If a building resembles another common object, it can take on a similar flow of chi energy. Ideally, the shape should have a positive image. If it is negative, such as the meat cleaver commonly associated with L-shaped buildings, you may need to take care with the allocation of rooms, and to compensate for a negative flow of chi energy. In the case of an L-shaped, "meat cleaver" building, for example, you would avoid placing bedrooms in the area of the "blade". Leafy plants placed in the "blade" area would also help.

One difficulty with this approach is that the significance of shapes is culturally biased: a tall shape might suggest a pole, a tree or a spear, so any general conclusions based on a single culture could be misleading.

MATERIALS AND SURFACES

Materials used on the interior and exterior walls of a building affect the speed of chi energy moving across the surfaces, which influences the ambient chi energy both inside and outside the home. In many districts, the exterior surfaces of the buildings will all be made of the same or similar materials – all brick, stone or timber – giving a particular emphasis to the chi energy of an entire neighbourhood.

More yang surfaces (see opposite) speed up chi energy and are especially typical of commercial buildings. More yin surfaces slow chi energy and are generally more suited to people's homes.

Problems can occur when a building with more yang surfaces, such as a modern steel and glass-fronted office block, is built in a residential neighbourhood. People in surrounding homes may begin to feel more tense, irritable and aggressive.

building materials

The ideal construction material in Feng Shui terms is one which allows healthy chi energy from the environment to pass easily into the building. The structure should also be damp-free – dampness leads to a heavy flow of chi energy, causing unhealthy stagnant pockets inside. Several materials are used for building and, like all other materials, they have different properties of yin and yang.

More yang materials, such as stone, tend to be both harder and more dense. When they are used for walls it is difficult for chi energy to pass through.

More yin materials, such as timber, allow energy to permeate the walls gently. A home with thick, hard stone walls is more isolated from the surrounding chi energy than one made of thin wooden planks. Brick or timber walls usually offer the best balance of yin and yang.

Synthetic materials, such as those used for insulation, are not good conductors of chi energy. Many plastics carry their own charge of static electricity and also partly insulate you from the flow of chi energy outside. Avoid them if practical.

Timber
This is the most yin building material. Wood originates from living plants, so in Feng Shui terms it is considered to be more alive than other materials. Dark hardwoods such as mahogany are more yang, whereas lighter softwoods such as pine are more yin.

Brick
Since they are made of clay, bricks are softer, slightly porous and therefore more yin than stone. Left bare, rough brick surfaces on interior walls slow chi energy and increase the risk of stagnation in internal corners. Plaster brick indoors to produce a smooth surface and promote a more balanced movement of chi energy.

Breeze block
A popular modern building material, breeze block is similar to brick but more yang. In itself it is not unfavourable, but the blocks have cavities that are often filled with synthetic insulating foam, which obstructs the flow of chi through the walls. Breeze-block buildings are usually cement-rendered on the outside and plastered on the inside, easing the flow of chi across the surface.

Stone
Hard stone such as granite is more yang then softer stone such as limestone. Uneven stone walls can scatter chi energy. Interior bare stone walls make chi bounce through a home in many directions, preventing stagnation. But stone is also less permeable than some other materials which can cause stagnation. Stone buildings should have large doors and windows to let in chi energy more easily.

Glass
Hard, shiny and flat, glass has mostly yang qualities, but it also allows chi energy in the form of light and radiated heat to flow easily into the home. A large expanse of glass will speed up the flow of chi energy along its surface. In residential buildings place plants and fabrics, such as curtains, close by large windows to slow the energy down.

EXTENSIONS AND INDENTATIONS

Few homes are completely rectangular. Most of them have either extensions, where parts of the building stick out, or indentations, where parts are "missing". To decide whether you have an extension or indentation, measure the width of your home in the relevant sector, then measure the part that sticks out and the "missing" part (see opposite). If the part that sticks out measures less than 50 per cent of the width it is an extension. If the "missing" part measures less than 50 per cent of the width, it is an indentation. Depending on their size and direction, extensions and indentations can be favourable or unfavourable.

ASSESSING THE EFFECTS

Generally, an extension will accentuate the type of chi energy in that part of the building; an indentation will diminish it. A large extension may exaggerate the chi energy too much, causing an imbalance. But whether an extension is only large enough to produce a healthy, rather than excessive, increase in the chi energy of that direction is a matter of judgment. The chart on pages 52–3 outlines the main problems and benefits you might expect from extensions and indentations in different directions. First decide whether you are, in fact, experiencing such problems. Changes in your life since you moved into the house may give you some useful clues.

Suppose, for example, there is an extension in the north-west of your home. This strengthens the chi energy associated with the head of the family. If all is well with the head of your family and his or her relationships with the rest of the the household, you can assume that any north-west extension is a beneficial size. On the other hand, if the head of your family is overbearing, causing problems for the rest of you, the north-west extension may be too large.

Indentations are normally considered to be unhelpful, but a small indentation can sometimes be an advantage. An indentation in the north, for example, will reduce the chi energy associated with spirituality, tranquillity and a quiet life, and this could be a temporary advantage for a young person embarking on a new career.

Where there appear to be problems, you can solve them in a variety of ways. A large mirror placed on the inside wall of an indentation can visually fill it by reflecting the rest of the room into it. Alternatively, plenty of plants placed outside the house inside the indentation itself will add their own chi energy to the missing sector and help smooth out uneven areas. A dense screen of bushy plants can also help create the illusion of walls. Using Five-Element remedies (see pages 28–9) and Eight Directions colours (see opposite) can also be effective.

solving problem extensions and indentations

Place the grid of the Eight Directions over your floor plan, matching centres, and align them (see pages 44–5). This will show you the direction of the extension or indentation. The chart overleaf outlines the problems and benefits linked with each one.

If you are having such problems, the chi energy of an extension would need to be calmed; that of an indentation would need to be boosted. Five-Element remedies can be used for both. Check the Five-Element chi energy of the relevant direction (see right) and add to the extension more of the Five-Element that drains that energy (see page 27) – an example is given on page 50. To boost the chi energy in an indentation, you need to place there more of the Five Element itself or a supportive Five Element. In a north-west indentation, for example, you would need to add more metal energy or more soil energy (which supports metal).

Alternatively, in decor and furnishings, use the Eight Directions colours associated with the relevant areas (see right) to boost indentations or calm extensions (see page 123).

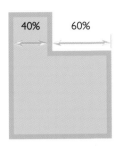

Extensions
If the part sticking out is less than 50% of the width of your home, it is an extension.

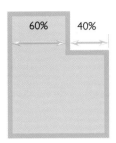

Indentations
If the "missing" part is less than 50% of the width of your home, it is an indentation.

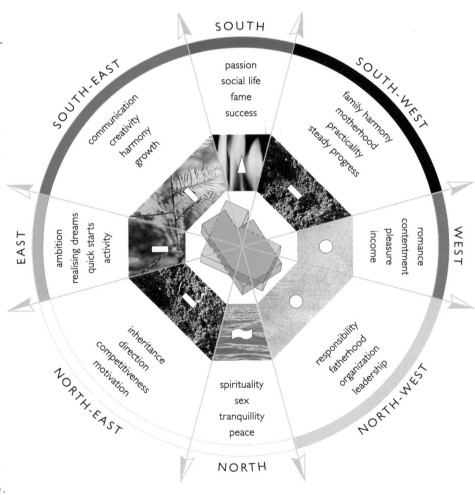

SOUTH
passion
social life
fame
success

SOUTH-EAST
communication
creativity
harmony
growth

SOUTH-WEST
family harmony
motherhood
practicality
steady progress

WEST
romance
contentment
pleasure
income

EAST
ambition
realising dreams
quick starts
activity

NORTH-WEST
responsibility
fatherhood
organization
leadership

NORTH-EAST
inheritance
direction
competitiveness
motivation

NORTH
spirituality
sex
tranquillity
peace

EFFECTS OF EXTENSIONS

NORTH

A **small extension** strengthens the chi energy associated with water, night and winter, creating a more peaceful, spiritual atmosphere in the home. It can make you quieter and more isolated, but also more self-sufficient and independent. Such buildings are most suited to older, more reclusive people. But they can also be beneficial for promoting fertility.

A **large extension here** could make your life too quiet, isolated and solitary. The problems caused by this can include loneliness, a drop in income and the possibility of sex scandals or sexually related illnesses.

NORTH-EAST

A **small extension** accentuates the chi energy linked to motivation, having a clear sense of direction and being prepared to work hard. But the unsettling chi energy of sudden changes is also stimulated, making these extensions generally undesirable.

A **large extension** can overwhelm the building with north-east chi energy, destabilizing the flow of chi throughout the home. It can lead to misfortune, and make you especially vulnerable to outside, possibly negative, spiritual influences. You may also become excessively materialistic and grasping.

EAST

A **small extension** encourages activity, favouring careers and business. It is particularly helpful for young people embarking on new careers and building up their lives, and for children, particularly the eldest son.

A **large extension** can generate a hyperactive atmosphere in which it is hard to wind down and relax. In your determined push for success you may rush things too much, and provoke setbacks. There may also be a tendency to become over-ambitious, which can lead to unrealistic expectations, and you eventually risk frustration and disappointment.

SOUTH-EAST

A **small extension** stimulates the chi energy associated with harmonious development. It encourages an active life, and is helpful in developing careers and businesses. In a family, a south-east extension favours daughters, especially for promoting an engagement or marriage. In general, buildings of this shape are favourable for prosperity and well-being.

A **large extension** can lead to excessive activity and eventually to ill-health. You risk becoming unable to develop your life harmoniously . You could become lazy, leading to diminishing success in your career or business.

EFFECTS OF INDENTATIONS

NORTH

This can **lower** the vitality of the people who live here, particularly their sexual energy. It is also associated with ill-health of reproductive organs, including problems with conception and fertility.

NORTH-EAST

A **small indentation** can sometimes be an advantage, though it is generally better to have a balanced shape.

A **large indentation** can lead to a loss of motivation, as well as to problems in starting a family. It may also have a detrimental effect on inheritance.

EAST

An **indentation** here produces problems for the children of the family, especially the eldest son. It can lead to a lack of ambition and drive, and weaken your ability to go out into the world and make things happen.

SOUTH-EAST

A **large indentation** can result in a drastic loss of harmonious chi energy, and can therefore lead to serious misfortune. It is not auspicious for the family's long-term future.

EFFECTS OF EXTENSIONS	EFFECTS OF INDENTATIONS

SOUTH

A small extension is favourable for fame, success and public recognition. It can also encourage you to be more passionate and outgoing, and promotes an active social life, particularly for anyone involved in public affairs.

A large extension can lead to inflated expectations and almost inevitable disappointment. It can also lead you to be unduly emotional and passionate, resulting in heated arguments and eventually to possible rifts with family and friends. It can be difficult to spend a lot of time comfortably in a home which suffers from an excess of the chi energy of the south.

SOUTH

An indentation here can make you more vulnerable to law suits and public prosecution. It can also have a dispiriting effect, leading to a loss of spontaneity and passion. It could be harder to attract attention or receive public recognition.

SOUTH-WEST

A small extension can promote family harmony and make you more practical and methodical. However, such extensions are along the same axis as the north-east although opposite it, and this can also destabilize the flow of chi energy in a similar way.

A large extension creates a powerful flow of chi energy supporting the mother or eldest woman. This can make her too dominant, to the detriment of the rest of the family. In the Far East, this type of house is sometimes called a widow's house, as the energy of the wife becomes too strong, exhausting her husband.

SOUTH-WEST

This weakens the chi energy associated with the mother or the eldest woman. It can lead to feelings of insecurity and jealousy and therefore family disharmony.

WEST

A small extension here can be good for enhancing your income and arranging loans, because the west is associated with the chi energy of the harvest. It also favours marriage, particularly for women, as it contributes to a more romantic atmosphere, and is ideal for entertaining and evening activities.

A large extension may lead to over-spending with the consequent loss of savings, and to an over-emphasis on the pursuit of pleasure. This could affect everyone in the family, but younger females would probably be most influenced by this tendency.

WEST

An indentation here can lead to discontent, which may affect the youngest daughter or woman in particular. A single woman living in such a building could find it more difficult to start a relationship, because the chi associated with romance is lacking.

NORTH-WEST

A small extension favours organization and planning ahead. It is beneficial for the steady building up of a career or business. It can help you pursue the top job in your chosen field, and to develop the fair sense of justice necessary for leadership. It enhances feelings of responsibility and is particularly supportive to the father or main wage-earner of the family.

A large extension could lead to the father or main wage-earner in the family becoming too powerful, making him or her arrogant, self-righteous, authoritarian and overbearing.

NORTH-WEST

An indentation here is unfavourable for the father or main wage-earner. This type of house is also known as a widow's house, because the lack of chi energy supporting the husband can weaken him and make him more vulnerable to illness.

BALANCING THE EIGHT TYPES OF CHI ENERGY

Generally, it is desirable to have an even balance of Eight Directions chi energies in your home. Circular and octagonal buildings are the most balanced shapes because there is an equal amount of chi energy in each of the Eight Directions. Totally circular and octagonal buildings are rare nowadays, although they were typical dwellings in the past. Rectangular buildings are much more common and the closer the rectangle is to a square, the more balanced are the eight types of chi energy. L-shaped houses or apartments can have the centre outside the building, so some types of chi energy would be completely missing. Other shapes, such as long narrow rectangles, can have very much more of some types of chi energy than others.

To assess the balance of chi energy in your home, place your grid of the Eight Directions over your floor plan as usual (see pages 44–5). This will indicate the deficient areas. Another approach is to consider any problems you or other occupants of the building may be having. If loneliness is a problem, for example, look at the northern part of your floor plan. If a large part of your home falls in that sector, it could be a possible cause. Information about previous occupants and their experiences in the home may also provide clues.

Ideally, imbalances in chi energy distribution should be corrected. especially if they appear to be causing difficulties for you or other members of your family. The process is similar to solving the problems of extensions and indentations (see pages 50–3). Where there are deficiencies, boost the relevant sector by placing in those areas objects that bring in more of the missing chi energy and of the supportive Five-Element chi energy (see pages 28–9).

EXPOSURE TO SUNLIGHT

Sunlight carries chi energy directly into your home, and the shape of the building can affect this process by enhancing its exposure to sunlight or reducing it. The size, position and number of windows are also significant. If part of a home is denied sun for all or much of the day, there is a serious risk of dampness and stagnating chi energy.

SHAPE

If an L-shaped building is orientated in a certain direction, part of it could be in shadow virtually all day long. Similarly, if a building has a north-facing indentation, none of those walls will be exposed to sunlight (see opposite). On the other hand, if the opening of an indentation faces the sun, the area becomes a sun trap attracting faster, more yang active chi energy, which is favourable.

Buildings receive most sunlight along their longer sides, so the directions of the long sides determine the type of sunlight and therefore the type of chi energy which will be most influential in your home. If the longest sides face east and west, for example, your home will be influenced mostly by sunrise and sunset. Assuming it has sufficient windows and is not overshadowed, the sunrise can energize your life so that you start up new projects, have lots of get up and go, and think positively in terms of a bright new future. Sunset, on the other hand, helps you to switch from the activity of the day to a more contented romantic mood.

NORTH-FACING WINDOWS

In apartments where all the windows face north, little direct sunlight can reach the interior, and they often have a cold cave-like atmosphere. The chi energy feels stagnant and there is a tendency to dampness. People living in such places could experience a host of problems including loneliness, feelings of isolation, lack of progress in their careers, a loss of vitality, depression and poor health.

If your home is affected in this way, it is important to explore means of bringing more chi energy into it. If possible put in skylights or south-facing windows. Failing this, introduce real fireplaces, keep lit candles especially in the north-east part of your home, grow plants (using daylight bulb since most plants are difficult to grow in such conditions) and keep the rooms relatively empty. It will also help to install wooden surfaces (for example, floors), hang mirrors, and place metal wind chimes in the west, north-west or north of your home.

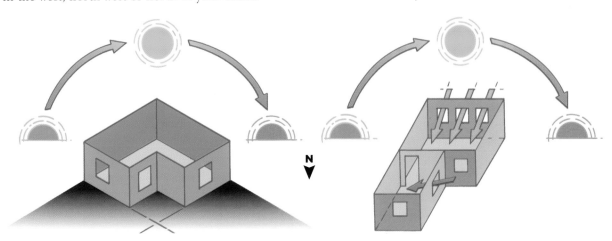

N

Poor exposure to sunlight
The L-shape of this house, its orientation and the north-facing windows all combine to prevent direct sunlight reaching the rooms for most of the day.

Good exposure to sunlight
This L-shaped building receives plenty of direct sunlight from the south through several south-facing windows. Though the north is in shadow for much of the day, the west-facing window in the extension lets in the afternoon sun.

the surroundings

A building's chi energy is strongly affected by its surroundings. Nearby structures, roads, and natural features all influence the chi energy moving past and into your home.

RURAL ENVIRONMENTS
▼

The principle of Five-Element shapes (see opposite) can also be applied to landscape. Decide which of the following elements best characterizes the landscape around you and check the chart overleaf for possible effects and solutions.

WATER Lakes, rivers, streams, marshes, seas.
TREE Trees, woods , forests.
FIRE Mountains with pointed peaks.
SOIL Plains, plateaux, meadows and generally flatter landscapes.
METAL Round rolling hills.

The chi energy of its environment affects your home in a variety of ways. Individual buildings and isolated features of the landscape such as water, trees and hills, as well as the overall character of the area where you live, can be significant.

Even the arrangement of streets is important from a Feng Shui perspective. In terraced housing, for example, people are grouped together in very similar homes, all orientated in the same direction. Many of the inhabitants sleep in the same direction. The same applies to other parallel streets. Close communities arise in these neighbourhoods because the people who live there have a lot in common. This is particularly so if the whole street is orientated in a generally beneficial direction. On roads running north-south, the houses face east and west; this is beneficial for both sides. However, if the streets run in an unhelpful direction, difficulties can be created for the whole community.

More modern housing estates have homes orientated in many directions and a greater choice of location. People are more likely to find homes that suit them specifically. Greater individualism, however, can lead to less community spirit. With such varied housing there is also more danger of cutting chi (see page 62).

In rural environments, buildings are spread out and there is often plenty of natural vegetation between them, so the distances between homes are too great to be significant.

NEIGHBOURING BUILDINGS

Certain types of building or other construction can adversely influence the chi energy of nearby homes. These include churches, graveyards, cemeteries, crematoriums, funeral parlours and hospitals, which all carry chi energy associated with suffering, illness, death and decay. Churches also carry the happy energy linked with weddings, christenings and festivals, which may well balance out the sad effects.

Other problem buildings are nuclear power stations and structures which emit high levels of electrical radiation (electrical substations housing mains voltage transformers, electrical pylons and buildings with a high consumption of electricity). Some of these are widely believed to carry specific health risks.

Ideally, none of these buildings should be close to or visible from your home. However, reactions to them are personal and many people find they can live near some of them with no ill effects.

five-element building shapes

Building shapes can be classified according to the type of Five-Element chi energy they generate (see below). Many buildings are a mixture of shapes and energies. A low building with a pointed roof, for example, combines soil and fire chi energy; a tall building with a dome encompasses tree and metal energies.

The Five Elements can be supportive or destructive to each other (see page 27), so the shapes of surrounding buildings can affect your home favourably or unfavourably. If your home has the same shape as its neighbours, it will be in harmony with them. But if it is a different shape, there could be problems and you will need to assess the potential effects. Decide first which of the Five-Element shapes your home most resembles, then which shapes the surrounding buildings resemble. The chart on pages 58–9 examines the possible combinationsof building shapes and outlines the potential effects on you and your neighbourhood.

Where the relationship between the shapes is inharmonious, the unfavourable consequences can be mitigated by employing Five-Element solutions. The chart gives the solutions, where necessary, and suggests means of implementing them. Other ways of putting Five-Element solutions into practice are described on pages 28–9. Choose one that is appropriate to your situation. Unless otherwise specifed, place the remedy between your home and the buildings with the problem shapes.

 ***Water***
Buildings that are irregular shapes, those that include many shapes (tall thin features, spires, domes or low rectangles) and those that are curved and flowing come into this category. They are often buildings that have been added to over the years.

Tree
Tall, thin rectangular buildings, such as modern high-rise offices or apartment blocks are tree-shaped. Churches with tall towers would also come into this category.

Fire
These are buildings with pointed roofs such as churches with spires, or with pyramid-shaped roofs, such as Canary Wharf in London and the Louvre pyramid in Paris.

Soil
Low, flat-roofed buildings or those with shallow sloping roofs are in this group. This is the shape of many ordinary houses and bungalows.

Metal
Round or domed buildings are metal-shaped. Those that have several arched or rounded features, such as arched cloisters, doorways and windows are also included.

FIVE-ELEMENT SHAPES	EFFECTS	SOLUTIONS
WATER surrounded by tree	The water chi energy of your home is drained by the tree energy of the surrounding buildings. This can lead to low vitality, anxiety and a decrease in sexual appetite.	Add metal or water energy (a metal ball, or water feature in the east or south-east).
WATER surrounded by fire	The water energy of your home destroys the fire energy of the surrounding buildings. This does not affect you directly, but it can create a less harmonious neighbourhood.	Add tree energy (tall green leafy plants and trees).
WATER surrounded by soil	The water energy of your home is destroyed by the soil energy of the surrounding buildings. You could feel anxious, fearful and constantly under attack.	Add metal energy (silver or gold-coloured metal balls or spheres).
WATER surrounded by metal	The water energy of your home is supported by the metal energy of the surrounding buildings. You should feel in harmony with your environment, independent, spiritual and with lots of vitality. It can also help you develop inner strength and flexibility.	
TREE surrounded by fire	The tree energy of your home is drained by the fire energy of the surrounding buildings. This can adversely affect the chi energy associated with activity, ambition and career-building.	Add water energy (a water feature in the east) and tree energy (tall plants or trees).
TREE surrounded by soil	The tree energy of your home destroys the soil energy of the surrounding buildings. This does not affect you directly but it can create an unsettled atmosphere in your neighbourhood.	Add fire energy (bright lights outside your home).
TREE surrounded by metal	The tree energy of your home is destroyed by the metal energy of the surrounding buildings. It could be difficult to find success in your career and to think positively about the future.	Add water energy (a water feature) in the east or south-east.
TREE surrounded by water	The tree energy of your home is supported by the water energy of the surrounding buildings. This is particularly favourable for careers. It can enhance ambition, making you more active and better able to put your ideas into practice.	
FIRE surrounded by soil	The fire energy of your home is drained by the soil energy of the surrounding buildings. This is detrimental to your chances of finding success and public recognition.	Add tree energy (tall plants) and fire energy (bright lights outside your home).
FIRE surrounded by metal	The fire energy of your home destroys the metal energy of the surrounding buildings. This will not harm you directly, but it could make your neighbourhood less prosperous.	Add soil energy (a low clay trough with rich black soil and spreading plants).

FIVE-ELEMENT SHAPES	EFFECTS	SOLUTIONS
FIRE surrounded by water	The fire energy of your home is destroyed by the water energy of the surrounding buildings. This could make you susceptible to public humiliation or hostile legal action.	Add tree energy (trees or tall plants).
FIRE surrounded by tree	The fire energy of your home is supported by the tree energy of the surrounding buildings. This could enhance your chances of attracting attention and lead to fame and public recognition for your work or achievements.	
SOIL surrounded by metal	The soil energy of your home is drained by the metal energy of the surrounding buildings. This can make you feel insecure and less settled, leading to problems with family relationships.	Add fire energy (bright exterior lights) and soil energy (low plants in a clay trough).
SOIL surrounded by water	The soil energy of your home destroys the water energy of the surrounding buildings. This may not affect you directly, but it could impair the vitality of your community generally.	Add metal energy (silvery or gold-coloured metal spheres).
SOIL surrounded by tree	The soil energy of your home is destroyed by the tree energy of the surrounding buildings. This can make you unsettled and insecure, leading to health problems especially for the mother.	Add fire energy (a real fire or wood-burning stove or bright lights) inside your home.
SOIL surrounded by fire	The soil energy of your home is supported by the fire energy of the surrounding buildings. This combination of chi energies is particularly favourable for creating a harmonious family atmosphere in your household.	
METAL surrounded by water	The metal energy of your home is drained by the water energy of the surrounding buildings. This is an unfavourable combination which can lead to financial problems.	Add soil energy (a clay trough with low spreading plants) and metal energy (metal spheres).
METAL surrounded by tree	The metal energy of your home destroys the tree energy of the surrounding buildings. This will not affect you directly, but it could affect your neighbours' ability to build up their careers.	Add water energy (a water feature) to the east or south-east of your home.
METAL surrounded by fire	The metal energy of your home is destroyed by the fire energy of the surrounding buildings. This can lead to financial hardship, and problems of over-indulgence, such as gambling.	Add soil energy (a clay trough with low spreading plants).
METAL surrounded by soil	The metal energy of your home is supported by the soil energy of the surrounding buildings. This is favourable for wealth creation and could help you build up your finances.	

SHADOWS

Sunlight brings energy into your home in the form of light, radiated heat, solar radiation and chi energy. As the sun moves through the sky it shines on different parts of your home's exterior, and in through the windows. If your home or apartment is denied the sun's energy, the chi energy there could stagnate, which can jeopardize the effectiveness of many Feng Shui solutions. Your home can be denied sunlight because of its shape or the number and position of its windows (see pages 54–5). Also, if your home is in the shadow of a taller neighbouring building, sunlight can be blocked out, obstructing the flow of chi energy into it.

When you are deciding whether to buy or lease a particular home, it is important to consider how it might be affected by shadows. Explore

directions of shadows

If part of your home is in shadow, chi energy of a particular kind will be lost. Which type it is depends on the position of the overshadowing building relative to your home. Shade from a particular location leads to a deficiency of the chi energy associated with that direction. For example, if there is a tall block to the east, you will be overshadowed when the sun is in the east and you will lack the chi energy of the east.

Luckily, there are a number of ways to remedy this. One is to add the colour linked with that direction (see page 31). Another is to reinforce the appropriate Five-Element chi energy (see pages 28–9).

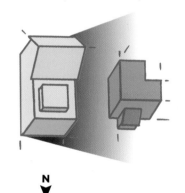

N

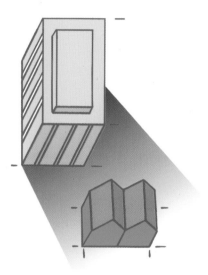

Shadows from the east
The chi energy associated with activity, ambition and building up your career will be deficient.

Solutions Enhance tree energy. Place a water feature – a fountain, pond or aquarium – east of the centre of your home either indoors or in the garden. Tall bright green plants and wooden surfaces are also helpful.

Shadows from the south-east
The chi energy associated with communication, creativity and harmonious progress will be deficient.

Solutions The Five-Element chi energy of the south-east is the same as that of the east so the solutions are similar. Place a water feature south-east of the centre of your home. Dark green and blue are helpful colours here. Tall plants and wooden surfaces are also supportive of tree energy and are therefore beneficial.

the surroundings of the building, and check whether there are any structures nearby which could cast shadows over your new home.

The important factors are the height of the neighbouring buildings, and their direction and distance from your home. A building to the east or west is more likely to overshadow you because the sun is lower in the sky in both these directions and casts longer shadows. You could be in shadow even if the structure is relatively low or some distance away from you. When the sun is high in the sky, it casts shorter shadows so a building in the south could be closer to you and not cause a problem.

In the northern hemisphere, buildings to the north will not cast a shadow over your home. If you live in the southern hemisphere, you will not need to worry about being overshadowed by buildings to the south.

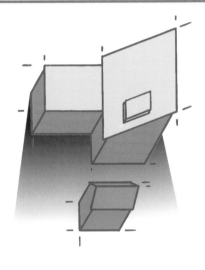

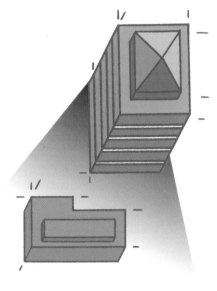

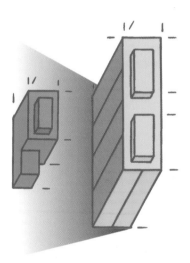

Shadows from the south
The chi energy associated with passion, public recognition and fame will be deficient.

Solutions Enhance fire energy. Install fireplaces or light candles. Place something purple south of the centre of your home. Tall plants with pointed leaves, particularly if they have purple leaves or flowers, and wooden surfaces will also help. Spiky objects or pointed patterns in decor or soft furnishings would also be helpful here.

Shadows from the south-west
The chi energy associated with consolidation, motherhood and family harmony will be deficient.

Solutions Enhance soil energy. Place candles or a fireplace to the south-west of the centre of your home. Something with the colour of rich black soil would help there, or a low spreading plant in an earthenware trough.

Shadows from the west
The chi energy associated with romance, contentment and income will be deficient.

Solutions Enhance metal energy. Place metal wind chimes or a shiny round metal plaque or silver or gold coins west of the centre of your home. A plant with round leaves and red flowers in a round silver pot will also be helpful.

Deflecting cutting chi
Reflective surfaces act as mirrors and deflect cutting chi away from your front door. The polished brass door-knob, letter box and the high-gloss paintwork would all be helpful.

CUTTING CHI

If the corner of a nearby building points at your home, your own building could be immersed in cutting chi (see page 14). This distorts the flow of your personal chi energy and that of other members of your household, making you feel unsettled and disorientated. The consequences of this can be serious, producing ill-health or causing you to lose your direction in life.

Cutting chi can enter your home through walls, but it gets in much more easily through windows and doors. Windows are less of a problem because people and other chi-carrying entities do not usually enter buildings this way. But if the corner of a nearby building is pointing at a door, especially the front door, the risk from cutting chi is more serious.

The location of the source of cutting chi is also significant since each direction carries a particular type of chi energy. The effects are particularly severe if the corner is to the north-east of your home because the chi energy in that direction is already sharp, piercing and prone to sudden changes. If this type of chi energy is stirred by an external corner, it can be much more damaging. The worst situation to deal with is a corner to the north-east of your home pointing straight at your front door.

EASING CUTTING CHI

To ease the effects of cutting chi you need to calm the flow of chi energy coming from the offending direction. You can do this very effectively by using the principles of the Five Elements – the support cycle in particular (see pages 28–9).

The Five-Element chi energy associated with a particular direction can be drained by the Five Element immediately following it in the support cycle: soil drains fire, metal drains soil, water drains metal, tree drains water, fire drains tree. This principle can be used as a tool to calm cutting chi. For example, suppose the source of the cutting chi is to the south-west of your home. The south-west is associated with soil chi energy, which is drained by metal chi energy. So to calm cutting chi from the south-west, you need to place an object linked with metal chi energy, such as a gold or silver disc, in the south-west of your home. Alternatively, place a large statue made of cast-iron, bronze or other metal, which includes circular shapes, in the garden between your house and the corner.

Simpler solutions would be to employ the universal remedies of Feng Shui. You could plant bushy trees and shrubs or a dense hedge between your home and the corner to absorb the harmful chi. Placing something shiny and reflective on your door will deflect cutting chi away. A mirror, shiny plaque or highly polished doorknob could all be effective.

ROADS

Cars, buses, and trucks and the people inside them travelling along roads all carry chi energy. They create fast-moving chi energy in themselves, and they also stir up the chi energy in the surroundings as they move along. Roads have hard flat surfaces, and are often constructed along straight lines, all of which is more yang and therefore generates an even faster flow of chi energy.

Roads that direct this fast-moving energy into your home upset the natural movement of chi energy there. If the road is busy and the traffic speeds along it, the flow of chi energy will be that much faster and more intense. These influences are further accentuated if your home is in certain positions: T-junctions, forks and bends in the road can all cause problems (see below). Occasionally apartment buildings are sited in the centre of a roundabout or ring of roads, which is a particularly vulnerable position.

The solutions are similar to those for cutting chi (see opposite); aim to slow down and subdue the flow of chi energy, and deflect some of it elsewhere. Plant bushy shrubs or place something reflective between your home and the road. Wind chimes hung in the hall or garden can help to cleanse and purify chi energy disturbed by nearby traffic.

FENG SHUI IN PRACTICE

Feeling unsettled at home
My first clients' home was at the head of a busy T-junction. They both felt restless there and found it difficult to relax. They avoided the rooms nearest the road and spent most of their time in the back of the house. The solution was to calm the flow of fast-moving chi from the road. I advised them to plant bushes in the front garden, place a convex mirror facing the road and to hang metal wind chimes inside the front door. Soon they felt much more settled, and were happy to spend more time at home.

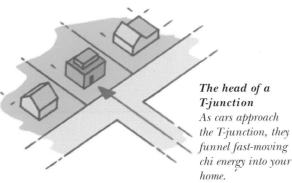

The head of a T-junction
As cars approach the T-junction, they funnel fast-moving chi energy into your home.

The outside of a bend
The bend induces fast-moving chi energy to spin away from the road. Buildings here will be affected by vehicles coming from both directions.

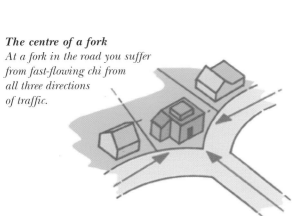

The centre of a fork
At a fork in the road you suffer from fast-flowing chi from all three directions of traffic.

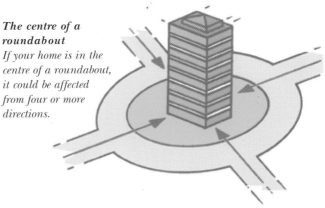

The centre of a roundabout
If your home is in the centre of a roundabout, it could be affected from four or more directions.

Yang water
A storm-tossed sea is more yang in two respects: the saltiness of the water and the violent motion of the waves.

WATER

In Feng Shui water has a special significance. It carries ingredients vital for human life, and is essential for growing our food. Human beings evolved from sea creatures, and most of our body weight is made up of water. But water can also be a threat in the form of floods and storms.

For many people, water holds a great attraction. Holidays, picnics and sporting activities often involve visiting places where there is water. Rivers, lakes, canals, waterfalls or swimming pools are regular features of many people's lives. In Feng Shui water represents money because money flows through a community in a similar way to the movement of water in a landscape.

Water near your home affects its chi energy, which in turn influences your own chi energy. When conditions are favourable, nearby water can enhance the chi energy of your home, thereby increasing your wealth and vitality. The important factors include the quality of the water, the way it flows, and its direction from the centre of your home.

The water itself must be clean, fresh and unpolluted. Dirty water is less able to enhance your vitality. Salt water from the sea or ocean is more yang, whereas fresh water from lakes, rivers and streams is more yin. Living near the sea is therefore more envigorating, and living by the side of a lake is more peaceful.

FLOWING WATER

The chi energy of moving water is more yang than that of still water, so a waterfall has a more active yang influence than a millpond. At the same time the downward movement of water creates a more grounding effect, whereas a bubbling spring has a more uplifting influence. A fast-flowing river moving in a straight line has a more yang, more focussed effect than a slow-moving stream that meanders through gentle curves. More yang fast-moving water speeds up the flow of chi energy in your home making it feel fresher, cleaner and more alive.

More yin slow-moving water leads to a gentler, more peaceful flow of chi energy. Ponds and bogs have the most yin influence, but are also most likely to become stagnant, creating stagnant chi energy. Stagnation can be avoided if the water contains a variety of thriving wildlife. Slow-moving water is also more susceptible to pollution, which takes longer to be washed away than it would in a fast-flowing mountain stream.

Water flowing towards the front door of your home brings more vitality into your home. Water flowing away from the entrance can carry vitality away. It can also lead to the feeling that wealth is flowing away from you. If the flow of water towards your home is too fast, it can cause a situation similar to cutting chi (see page 62).

solving problems of water directions

The location of water in relation to the centre of your home determines its effects. Align the grid of the Eight Directions with your floor plan to assess the direction of any water near of your home (see pages 44–5). The solutions to unfavourable locations involve harmonizing Five-Element chi energies.

South-east – favourable
Water here supports the tree energy of the south-east, which favours communication, creativity and harmonious development. The effect is similar to, though gentler than, water in the east.

South – unfavourable
Water does not mix well with the fire energy here. There is a risk of law suits, loss of reputation and poor health.

Solution Build up tree energy by planting tall trees between your home and the water.

South-west – unfavourable
Water here is destroyed by soil energy. In Oriental medicine water energy is associated with your kidneys, which are considered to be the source of chi energy in the body, so if they are harmed it can lead to serious illness.

Solution Build up metal energy as for the north-east.

East – favourable
The east carries tree energy, which is supported by water. It is good for career-building, being active and realising your dreams.

West – unfavourable
Water here drains metal energy, which can lead to problems with money and in finding romance.

Solution Build up metal chi energy as in the north-east or soil chi energy. A low mound of earth with a black pebble on top between the water and your home would be ideal.

North-east – unfavourable
This is least desirable direction because water energy here is destroyed by soil energy. The chi energy of the north-east is quick-changing, and fast-flowing water can lead to instability and unexpected changes in your life. Your health could also be at risk.

Solution Build up metal energy by placing something round and made of iron between the water and your home. Something red will also help. If iron is unsuitable use another metal.

North – unfavourable
Water here has a neutral effect. Even so, it is not recommended because the chi energy of the north is cold, quiet and still which makes it difficult to get rid of dampness. Constant dampness can lead to illnesses.

Solution Plant tall trees between your home and the water. The trees will absorb water literally, as well as water chi energy.

North-west – unfavourable
Water here drains metal energy, which can lead to the feeling that you are not in charge of your life.

Solution Build up metal chi energy as given for the north-east. Place something silver or white between the water and your home.

SOUTH
SOUTH-EAST
SOUTH-WEST
EAST
WEST
NORTH-EAST
NORTH-WEST
NORTH

HILLS

When choosing a home in the countryside, or a plot on which to build, its position in relation to hills in the surrounding landscape is important in Feng Shui terms.

If the building is on a hill, check whether it is the more yang sunny side, or the more yin shady side. A building on the sunny side of a mountain increases your exposure to the sun's energy and is usually preferable. On the shady side you risk the chi energy in your home stagnating. Ideally, the front of the house should face away from the slope so that the mountain rises behind the building. If your home is on the sunny side, the front will face south-east, south, or south-west in the northern hemisphere. Of these south-east would be most desirable and south-west least desirable. In the southern hemisphere, it will be facing north-east, north and north-west. Of these north-east is the most desirable, north-west the least.

The closer you are to the top of a mountain, the more you will be influenced by quicker, more yang chi energy, and the likelier you are to lead a more yang, active life style. The closer you are to the bottom of the slope or valley floor, the more you will be influenced by more yin slow-moving chi energy. A location about half-way up the slope produces the most advantageous balance.

The shape of the hills is also important. Sharp rocky mountains are more yang, and represent Five-Element fire chi energy. Round rolling hills are more yin, and relate to metal chi energy. Low flat-topped hills represent soil chi energy

TREES

Trees bring more Five-Element tree chi energy to an area but since they soak up water through the roots, they also drain water chi energy. In wooded areas, both the shape and position of trees are important.

If tall trees are too close to your home, they can overshadow you in the same way that tall buildings can (see pages 60–1). In the northern hemisphere, trees to the north are beneficial because they do not overshadow you and are in harmony with water chi energy. In the southern hemisphere, the same is true of trees to the south.

Tree and leaf shapes are significant. Tall trees with spiky needles, such as pines, or with long pointed leaves, such as palms, represent fire chi energy, and create a quicker more yang flow of chi energy than do broader bushy trees with more rounded leaves.

Trees can also have symbolic value. Evergreen trees, for example, signify long life. Trees or shrubs with sharp thorns can cause problems if they are too close to the house, since they can produce cutting chi.

the ROOMS in your HOME

If you place rooms in favourable

locations and choose your

furnishings and decor

according to Feng Shui

principles, it can make you

happier and more comfortable

in your home, and generally

further your aims in life.

allocating rooms

The direction of a room from the centre of your home determines its chi energy. Different types of activity benefit from different types of energy, so allocating rooms to favourable locations not only makes you more comfortable but can further your aims in life.

Before allocating a room to a location in your home think about the activities that will take place in the room most of the time. The kitchen, for example, is mainly the place where you prepare meals, the living room is where you relax and entertain guests, the dining room is where you eat, the bedroom is where you sleep and the study is where you work. Then decide which kind of chi energy will best support these activities. Ideally, each room should be located in a direction that will provide the most favourable type of chi energy for its main activity.

Of course, it is not always possible to achieve ideal solutions. Even if you build a completely new home, budget considerations or the limitations of the site will invariably mean that you have to modify your plan for an ideal Feng Shui environment. If your home is already built or you live in rented accommodation, you may be even more limited in your choices. But part of the art of Feng Shui is to enable you to encourage the most advantageous flow of chi energy whatever the practicalities of your particular situation.

YOUR PERSONAL NEEDS

Different people look for different qualities in particular rooms, depending partly on taste but also on the kinds of ambience they find most sympathetic for the various activities in their lives. So if a room's energy is to be helpful to you, it is important to take your own particular needs into account when you allocate rooms to particular locations. A living room in the north of your home, for example, will have a very different atmosphere from one in the south. The former will be quiet and still, the latter warm and fiery. Which of these qualities would be most helpful to you? If you are living a stressful life working hard and far into the evening, you may want a living room that is more tranquil than most, in which case a northern location would be more favourable. If you often have visitors, you may want the more social energy you would get from a living room in the south.

To take another example, if you generally sleep well but find you lack energy during the day, it may be that your bedroom's chi energy is too quiet for you and that a more active environment would be preferable. In this case a bedroom in the east or south-east of your home would be better. On the other hand, if you have plenty of energy in the day but are restless at night, you could benefit from a more peaceful room to sleep in and a northern bedroom would be more suitable.

WHICH ROOM FOR WHICH FUNCTION

To allocate rooms to the most favourable locations in accordance with your particular needs, it is helpful to understand the natural flow of chi energy through your home, and then how to adjust the flow so that it becomes more harmonious.

In deciding which location has the most favourable flow of chi energy for a particular function, you need to take account of the principles of yin and yang (pages 70–1), the Five Elements (pages 72–3) and the Eight Directions (pages 74–5). Applying these concepts to your home you should be able to place functions in spaces in a way that works for you rather than against you.

To begin with, consider each concept separately and digest its implications for the allocation of rooms before going on to the next one. Start with the simplest principle, which is yin and yang, then go on to the Five Elements and finally the Eight Directions. With experience you will be able to consider all three simultaneously.

ASSESSING YOUR FLOOR PLAN

First draw up an accurate floor plan of your home following the directions on pages 42–3. If your home covers more than one floor, make a separate plan of each floor. Lay the grid of the Eight Directions over each floor in turn and align them (pages 44–6). This will show you the precise direction of each room from the centre of your home.

In some cases, a room may have more than one direction passing through it; for example, it could be partly south and partly south-east of the centre. In cases like this, the part of the room that is in the south-east segment will have the typically active tree chi energy of the south-east, and the part that is in the south will have the characteristically spontaneous fire chi energy of the south.

ASSESSING EACH ROOM

Your understanding of the pattern of chi energy in your home can be further refined by looking at each individual room. Whatever the direction of a room from the centre of your home, there are also differences in parts of the room which could be relevant in some cases. The northern part of a room, for example, is more yin than the southern part; and the directions within a room carry some of the characteristics of the chi energy of the Five Elements and the Eight Directions. This can be particularly useful where, as is often the case, a room has to serve more than one function, as in a kitchen/dining room or a living room/dining room. It means you can fine-tune the allocation of space to the various activities that go on there, and furnish and decorate accordingly.

Rooms with two functions
Where a room serves more than one function, as in a kitchen/dining room, you need to assess the chi energy in each part of the room in order to allocate the functions harmoniously within the room.

USING YIN AND YANG

If you live in the northern hemisphere, the yang sunny side of your home is in the south-east, south and south-west, and the yin shady side is in the north-west, north and north-east (see also pages 18–19). For those living in the southern hemisphere, the shady side is in the south and the sunny side the north.

South and north are the extremes of yang and yin respectively. The east, where the sun rises, reflects the active nature of everything and is therefore more yang; the west, where the sun sets, is more passive, more yin. Beginning in the north, the most yin direction (associated with the middle of the night and the middle of winter), and moving clockwise through north-east, east and south-east, each direction becomes progressively more yang until you reach the south, the most yang. Continuing through south-west, west and north-west, the directions become progressively more yin until you reach north, the most yin. Although north and south are extremes, neither is completely yin or completely yang. Each always has elements of the opposite.

Take the floor plan of your home, with the grid of the Eight Directions placed over it, and relate the principle of yin and yang to the the directions of the rooms. This will show you which of the rooms are more or less yin or yang, giving you a basis for allocating functions to rooms harmoniously.

NATURAL BALANCE

When you are at home it often happens that you instinctively gravitate to a direction that is beneficial for you at a particular moment. If you have had a stressful yang day at work, for example, you may find that somewhere more yin and quiet in the northern part of your home will help you to unwind and relax. If you are studying at home and need a break, you may wander into a more yang active part of your home in search of extra stimulation. By making yourself aware of the qualities of yin and yang in different areas of your home, you can develop this natural balance more consciously.

YIN AND YANG ACTIVITIES

First, list all the activities that happen in your home. These might include cooking, eating, bathing, sleeping, sex, work, listening to music, watching television, relaxing and so on. Next decide whether these activities would be helped by a more yin or more yang environment, and rank them in order from the most yang to the most yin. Use your personal needs, rather than any objective assessment, to determine the ranking of each activity. If you want to be able to relax more while you

MORE YANG ACTIVITIES

Physical exercise
Work
Parties
Cooking
Hobbies
Housework
Mending things
Playing music
Studying
Painting
Entertaining
Bathing
Sex
Reading
Listening to music
Watching TV
Relaxation
Meditation
Sleeping

MORE YIN ACTIVITIES

are working, for example, then work will be lower down the list. On the other hand, if you want to wake yourself up while you are working, it will be higher. An example of such a list is shown on page 70.

YIN AND YANG ROOMS

The next step is to list types of room from yang to yin, considering the activities that take place in them. You will probably need to put some more or less compatible activities together in the same room – sleeping and sex in the bedroom, for instance, or listening to music and entertaining in the living room. It all depends on your lifestyle and on how many rooms you have. An example of such a list is shown right. To demonstrate the principle of allocating rooms, it includes more separate rooms than would be normally found in an average home.

Finally, place each type of room as far as possible in an appropriate direction: the most yang rooms in the most yang positions and the most yin rooms in the most yin positions. An important consideration is the exposure of the rooms to sunlight. For yang rooms to be most effective, the sun's yang energy must be able to enter the room directly. If there are no windows, the sun's chi energy will still enter the room but not with the same strength.

Practical considerations, such as the need to locate the kitchen, bathroom and utility room close to each other because they share water supply and drainage facilities, may also require modifications to your plans. The rooms in the list might be arranged as shown below.

MORE YANG ROOMS

Study/office
Living room
Kitchen
Workshop
Utility room
Dining room
Television room
Bathroom
Bedrooms
Store cupboards

MORE YIN ROOMS

A yin-yang floor plan
1 North *Bedroom, television room*
2 North-east *Store cupboards*
3 East *Bathroom, study/office*
4 South-east *Kitchen, utility room*
5 South *Living room*
6 South-west *Workshop*
7 West *Dining room*
8 North-west *Bedroom*

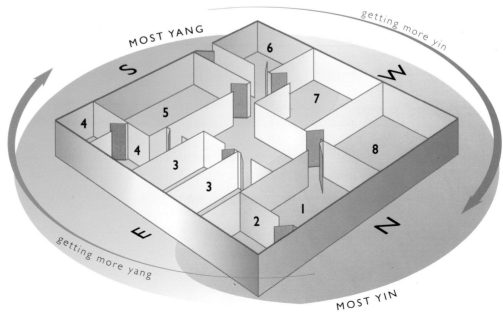

MOST YANG

getting more yin

getting more yang

MOST YIN

USING THE FIVE ELEMENTS

Like yin and yang, the Five Elements – water, tree, fire, metal, soil (see pages 24–9) – are related to the way the sun moves through the sky. They are also linked with the Eight Directions. Each type of Five-Element chi energy promotes certain qualities and works against others. Depending on your or your family's individual needs, these qualities can help you with certain types of activity or hinder you. The chart opposite lays out the pros and cons. You can use this knowledge to help you allocate the rooms in your home more harmoniously.

HOW TO ALLOCATE THE ROOMS

First note the direction of each room using the Eight Directions grid over the floor plan and check the kind of Five-Element chi energy present in that direction (opposite). Use the chart to decide whether a room's energy will be helpful for the kinds of activity you have in mind for it. Allocate the rooms accordingly and so that you spend most of your time in the chi energy that best suits you. In other words, it is more important for rooms where you spend a great deal of time to be located harmoniously, than rooms which you use only occasionally.

Suppose, for example, you want to get ahead in your career. Uplifting tree chi energy might be the most helpful to you. This is located to the east and south-east. If you work from home, place your office or workroom in the east or south-east so that you benefit from tree energy while you work. If you work outside the home, place your bedroom there, so that you benefit from tree energy while you sleep.

HARMONIZING WATER AND FIRE

Before finalizing your allocation of rooms, check that water and fire are in harmony with Five-Element chi energy. In kitchens and bathrooms, in particular, where water and fire are present in their pure forms, it is essential that they mix harmoniously to ensure that beneficial influences are carried throughout the home. If they are antagonistic, the flow of energy will be disturbed and disharmony will spread to other parts of the house (see also pages 103 and 107).

Water mixes most harmoniously with the tree energy of the east and south-east. So these are the most suitable directions for a bathroom. Fire mixes most harmoniously with the tree energy of the east and south-east and with the soil energy of the north-east and south-west. So the east and south-east are also the best positions for a kitchen, because both fire and water are present. Where a room is not in an ideal location, you can use Five-Element solutions to adjust the unfavourable chi energy. This is explained further on pages 106 and 110).

FIVE ELEMENT	PROMOTES	HELPFUL FOR	WORKS AGAINST	RISKS
WATER North	Inner development Tranquillity Spirituality Sexual activity Sleep Independence Objective thinking Being affectionate Conception	Elderly people Stress Insomnia Convalescence Ill-health Sexual problems	Activity Expression Passion Business	Too quiet Isolation Loneliness
TREE East /South-east	New projects Career Quick starts Activity Being busy Ambition Concentration Initiative	Young people Rebuilding a career Lack of confidence Lack of drive Needing a new start Lethargy	Romance Relaxation Patience Stability Security Contentment Slowing down	Over-ambition Workaholism Inability to relax Hyperactivity

FIRE
South
	Passion
	Expression
	Fame
	Parties
	Mental stimulation
	New ideas
	Sociability
	Spontaneity
		Adults
		Inability to meet
		  people
		Feelings of life
		  passing you by
		Lack of inspiration
		Isolation
		Shyness
			Relaxation
			Concentration
			Attention to detail
			Objective thinking
			Emotional stability
			Calm relationships
				Stress
				Arguments
				Separation
				Excess emotion

SOIL South-west/Centre/ North-east	Stability Steady progress Security Caring Family harmony Nurturing Motherhood Home Caution Methodical thinking	Early middle age Starting a family Family quarrels Being too impulsive Taking too many risks	Quick-thinking Ambition Dynamism Spontaneity New career New business	Becoming slow Getting in a rut Boredom
METAL West/North-west	Planning ahead Finances Leadership Organization Finishing things Business Budgeting	Later middle age Being disorganized Inability to plan ahead Lack of control Lack of self-discipline Inability to finish things	Dynamism Expression Showing feelings Being outgoing Starting projects	Being anti-social Introversion Self-repression

USING THE EIGHT DIRECTIONS

The Eight Directions are a further refinement of yin and yang and the Five Elements, and provide eight different kinds of chi energy to take into account. There is also the centre, which has its own characteristics, and which, in terms of positioning rooms, is usually kept as empty as possible. As with the Five Elements, the chi energy in each of the Eight Directions entails both benefits and potential risks. These are described in full on pages 30–3, but the chart opposite provides a useful quick guide for the purpose of allocating rooms.

HOW TO ALLOCATE THE ROOMS

Note the direction of each room using the Eight Directions grid over your floor plan. Then use the chart opposite to assess the type of chi energy in each room. There are several approaches you can take to allocating the rooms. You can match the room's activities to areas with supportive chi energy, or you can target areas of your life you wish to improve, identify the kind of chi energy that will be helpful and allocate the rooms so that you spend most of your time there, or you can use the Eight Directions to solve a particular problem.

Suppose, for example, you feel lonely quite a lot of the time. Check your floor plan to see if there is anything in the arrangement of rooms that might explain it. Perhaps your bedroom is in the north of your home. If the head of your bed is also pointing north, this intensifies the chi energy of the north, which carries a risk of isolation and loneliness. A more favourable position for the bedroom would be the south-east because the chi energy there promotes communication and the ability to make friends. The more time you can spend there, the better. Move your bedroom to the south-east and turn your bed so that the top of your head also points south-east; sleep there for at least three months then review any changes in your life.

IMPROVING YOUR LIFE

By a similar process of deduction, you can make definite improvements in your life and that of your family. Maybe, for example, you find that you are edgy, irritable and tense quite a lot of the time. This is becoming a problem for you and your family and you would like to be able to relax more easily, and to become more serene.

Reading the chart opposite you will see that the north-east and south would be problematical directions for you, both being restless, rather active positions. It would be wise to avoid spending a great deal of time in that part of your home. If possible, position your bedroom in the west where the chi energy is much more settled and contented.

DIRECTION	PROMOTES	RISKS
NORTH	Tranquillity More flexible attitudes Greater independence Creativity Inner growth Spiritual awareness	Isolation Loneliness Unnecessary worrying Greater insecurity Business or career becoming quiet Losing the desire to go out
NORTH-EAST	Self-motivation Competitiveness Sharper direction in life Inheritance Desire to work hard	Rushing into situations Becoming greedy Becoming more selfish Insomnia and nightmares Feeling on edge
EAST	Quick start to career or business Attention to detail Becoming more active Self-confidence and optimism Putting ideas into practice Realising your dreams in life Ambition	Being too ambitious Trying to do too many things Not completing tasks Being too career-orientated Exhaustion through over-activity Carelessness Impatience
SOUTH-EAST	Creativity Communication More harmonious progress Travel opportunities	Becoming too persistent Less able to take criticism Tiredness from lack of rest
SOUTH	Passion Active social life Being noticed Public recognition	Stressful life style Big emotional swings Separation Argumentativeness
SOUTH-WEST	Family harmony and motherhood Slow steady progress Saving money/thrift Deep friendships	Slow progress in career/business Dependence on others Cautiousness
WEST	Making money Romantic feelings Contentedness Pleasures and entertainment	Over-spending Loss of motivation Obsession with pleasures
NORTH-WEST	Leadership qualities Ability to organize Taking on responsibility Wisdom Commanding respect and trust	Self-righteousness Becoming authoritarian Overly controlling of others Arrogance

problem features

Regardless of their location in your home, certain features always have a negative effect on chi energy. Some of them are structural features which may be difficult, expensive or simply impossible to eradicate, especially if you are living in a rented apartment.

Fortunately, even if your home suffers from several of these defects, their negative effects can be mitigated by employing some simple Feng Shui solutions. Large plants, spotlights and mirrors are especially effective in such cases.

Protruding corners
Corners thrusting into a room are a cause of cutting chi (see page 14), and can have a disorientating influence on anyone sitting or sleeping nearby. This quick-swirling cutting chi needs to be calmed.

Solution Place a large plant on the floor or hang a basket of trailing plants in front of the corner. Plants soften the sharpness and, more importantly, have their own field of chi energy that slows the flow of cutting chi passing through them from the corner. A more yin plant with round floppy leaves is the best choice. Alternatively, drape a curtain in front of the corner.

Internal corners
Chi energy tends to stagnate in internal corners. They also harbour dust, which is another warning of possible stagnation.

Solution Speed up the flow of chi energy using plants, hard shiny surfaces or spotlights. Plants with pointed leaves are the most effective. Alternatively, hang a tall mirror in the corner, or a crystal so that

the light from the room refracts through it into the corner. A spotlight directed into it adds energy and light. Sound can also keep chi energy moving. This could be music or even a bell. In our living room we have a corner which is also under a sloping ceiling. We put plenty of plants in the corner and also an old-fashioned telephone with a bell. Every time it rings it stimulates the movement of chi energy there.

Clutter *Untidiness slows the flow of chi energy and greatly increases the risk of stagnation.*

Solution Keep your home neat and clean. Store as much as possible and keep cupboards and storage areas well-ordered. A major clear-out and reorganization of these areas from time to time can have a revitalizing effect on the flow of chi. Have a thorough house-cleaning in spring and summer.

No natural light *Any room without natural light is problematical in Feng Shui terms as natural light is one of the main mediums for keeping chi energy moving. Internal bathrooms and basement rooms are the most likely to present this problem.*

Solution Use daylight bulbs and candles, and grow plants like ivy, which will tolerate a minimum of light.

Sloping ceilings
These compress the chi energy below them and create a more intense atmosphere. The effect is strengthened if the ceiling is low.

Solution Keep chi energy moving upwards and away from the area below the slope. Anything that creates an illusion of greater height will help. Shine uplighters on to the ceiling, or place tall plants under the slope to introduce more upward-moving energy.

Beams
Structural beams can be made of various materials such as concrete, wood, or steel and may be exposed or hidden. Some support the weight of one or more upper floors. Beams can negatively affect chi energy. If the edges are sharp, exposed beams also bring cutting chi into a room. Concrete beams often have sharp edges; whereas wooden beams, especially old ones, are likely to be more rounded. which makes them potentially less of a problem. Steel beams, in particular, distort the flow of chi and are more damaging than wooden beams. The most harmful influence will be exerted by a large steel beam carrying the weight of several floors. This creates a feeling of pressure for people living below it. The height of beams is also significant: the higher the ceiling the weaker the influence of any beam. It is always better to avoid sleeping under beams, but particularly under an exposed, sharp-edged steel beam, because the distorted flow of energy is not conducive to good health.

Solution The remedies are similar to those for sloping ceilings. Use uplighters and tall, leafy plants with round bushy leaves to relieve the distortion.

L-shaped rooms
Not only will an L-shaped room have cutting chi from the protruding corner, but it is also an unbalanced shape in Feng Shui terms.

Solution To create the impression of more balanced proportions, place a mirror in the narrow part to make the space there seem twice as wide (see page 149).

simple feng shui remedies

If the chi energy in a room is unsatisfactory for the activities that take place there, it may be impractical for the time being to implement any radical solutions such as redecorating or relocating rooms.

In such cases there are some very simple remedies that can be used. First, check the room's location.

If the direction is unfavourable for its function, you need to decide whether the chi energy there needs to be enhanced or calmed. If the chi energy is favourable you can simply help to maintain that beneficial balance. Check the direction on the chart below and apply the appropriate remedy.

DIRECTION	ENHANCE CHI	MAINTAIN CHI	CALM CHI
NORTH	Round silver or iron pot filled with red flowers or a red flowering plant.	Grow ivy or water lilies with white plants. Curved glass statue or crystal.	Tall plants.
NORTH-EAST	Candles.	White flowers in low clay container.	Sea salt in small round white china bowl.
EAST	Water feature.	Tall plants.	Candles.
SOUTH-EAST	Water feature.	Tall plants.	Candles.
SOUTH	Tall plants.	Candles.	Charcoal in a low clay pot.
SOUTH-WEST	Candles.	Charcoal in a low clay pot.	Sea salt in a small round white bowl.
WEST	Charcoal in a low clay pot.	Red flowers in a round iron pot. Metal wind chimes or clock.	Grow ivy or water lilies. Curved glass statue or crystal.
NORTH-WEST	Charcoal in a low clay pot.	White flowers in a round silver pot. Metal wind chimes or clock.	Grow ivy or water lilies. Curved glass statue or crystal.
CENTRE	Keep empty.	Keep empty.	Keep empty.

the living room

The living room is central to family life and supports probably the widest range of activities of any room in the home. It is where you entertain your guests, host parties and hold important family celebrations. It is also, often, the place where you relax after a day's work and maybe read a book, watch television or listen to music.

Usually the living room is the largest room, and plenty of space is essential to its success. Chi energy can stagnate in overcrowded, claustrophobic rooms. If your potential living room is too small, open out two or more adjoining rooms. It is easier to keep chi energy flowing gently through one large room than through several small ones. Use mirrors where necessary, to adjust the overall proportions of the room and create an illusion of space (see page 149). Long thin rooms and L-shaped rooms can both be improved in this way.

A fireplace is often the focal point in a living room. Because of its association with Five-Element fire energy, it presents both opportunities and risks, and requires careful consideration (see page 83). But the most important item of furniture is the seating. How you arrange the chairs and sofas affects the ambience of the entire room (see pages 84–5).

LIVING/DINING ROOMS

Often, particularly in small apartments, it is practical to combine the living room and dining room. Generally, entertaining and eating are compatible functions, and you can usually create an atmosphere that works for both. Sometimes, the living and dining area also incorporates the kitchen. The main drawback here is that the kitchen part must be kept especially clean and tidy at all times. If not, it has a negative impact on chi energy which can spread to the rest of the room. (See pages 87–92 and 103–6 for considerations affecting dining rooms and kitchens.)

FAVOURABLE LOCATIONS

A bright sunny room will help to create a lively uplifting place where you and your family will enjoy spending time together. The sunlight charges up the chi energy and helps to stimulate the flow of energy through the room. Ideal positions are south-east, south, south-west and west of the centre of your home. South-east is bright and lively. South is favourable for holding parties and large social events. South-west will help create a settled cosy atmosphere. West is good for entertaining and the pursuit of pleasure generally; it also has a romantic character.

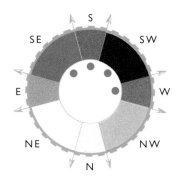

Recommended directions for a living room
South-east, south, south-west and west of the centre of your home.

an ideal living room

The south-east is one of the favourable locations for a living room and is characterized by lively, uplifting tree energy. Use furnishings and decor to enhance the room's spaciousness and to make it feel relaxing and comfortable. At the same time, try to promote sociability and family harmony. To allow chi energy to circulate freely, keep large pieces of furniture to a minimum and do not overuse heavy fabrics and upholstery. Balance the need for comfort against the risk of chi energy stagnating.

① LIGHTING *The vertical direction of uplighters and standing lamps supports tree energy, adding to the upward-moving atmosphere.*

② TELEVISION *Electronic equipment has a negative effect on chi energy. Position the television away from the seating, and ensure that people watching can sit in favourable directions in the room (see page 86), especially if they watch for more than a few hours a week.*

③ PLANTS *The negative effects of the television are minimized by living plants nearby. The tall palm supports tree energy, though spiky pointed leaves are not usually recommended in living rooms (see below). In smaller rooms, round-leaved bushy plants would be more appropriate.*

④ SOFAS AND CHAIRS *Arrange seating to promote sociability and family harmony (see pages 84–5). Sofas and chairs placed north-west facing south-east and west facing east are the most favourable positions in this room (see page 86). To promote relaxation, choose living room seating which is more yin – soft and rounded. Rounded shapes also avoid cutting chi. Green and cream are harmonious in the south-east – the more yin pale green helps create a feeling of airy spaciousness.*

⑤ FLOOR COVERING *The stripped wooden floor supports tree energy and generally maintains the harmonious flow of chi energy in the room. The pure wool rug provides comfort while avoiding the risks of stagnation that a fitted carpet would present.*

⑥ WINDOW TREATMENT *Fabrics help slow chi energy, which is relaxing and appropriate to a living room. But curtains should not be too full here, as this risks stagnation.*

⑦ WALL COVERING *Vertical stripes support tree energy and, like uplighters, help to create an impression of height and space. Patterned walls are more yin than plain walls, ideal in a living room where relaxation and comfort are important goals.*

⑧ PAINTINGS *Cheerful subjects such as a brilliant sunrise have positive psychological effects.*

⑨ ACCESSORIES *Choose colours for accessories such as cushions to fine-tune chi energy. Purple calms tree energy in a south-east room.*

Five-Element remedies
If the energy in the room feels stagnant, a water feature will boost favourable chi, especially if placed in the south-east part of the room.

THINGS TO AVOID IN A LIVING ROOM

SPIKY PLANTS Sharp-pointed leaves produce cutting chi, so plants like palms and yuccas should not be used in living rooms unless there is plenty of space and they can be kept apart from seating areas (see pages 84-5).

CLUTTER To prevent chi energy stagnating, keep living rooms free of household clutter and too many decorative objects. The centre of the room should be relatively empty.

CLOSED CURTAINS To allow energizing sunlight freely into the room, keep curtains wide open during the day, exposing the entire window.

OVER-FURNISHING Chi energy needs space to move; keep furniture to a minimum.

PROTRUDING CORNERS If exposed these can cause cutting chi, so screen them with tall bushy plants or drape them with fabric.

A living room in the south-east
Many of the room's decorative features support the upward tree energy here.

FRENCH DOORS

INTERNAL DOOR

CHOOSING THE DECOR

In a south-east living room colours and patterns should aim to maintain the favourable lively chi energy. Dark green is a harmonious colour, but paler more yin shades are also used to promote relaxation and give the room a light spacious feel. To calm the chi energy here, use more pale purple; to build it up use more cream and off-white. Shades of blue could be used instead of, or in addition to, green. Vertical patterns such as stripes in green and cream support tree energy. Irregular patterns would be enhancing, pointed ones calming.

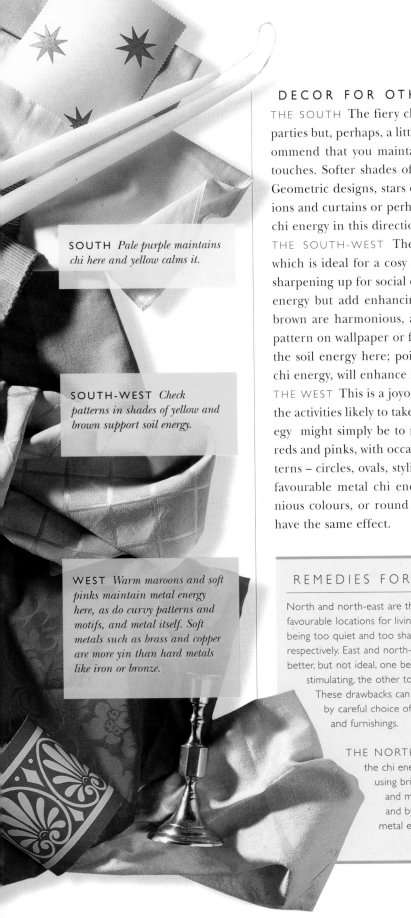

SOUTH *Pale purple maintains chi here and yellow calms it.*

SOUTH-WEST *Check patterns in shades of yellow and brown support soil energy.*

WEST *Warm maroons and soft pinks maintain metal energy here, as do curvy patterns and motifs, and metal itself. Soft metals such as brass and copper are more yin than hard metals like iron or bronze.*

DECOR FOR OTHER FAVOURABLE LOCATIONS

THE SOUTH The fiery chi energy here is warm and sociable, ideal for parties but, perhaps, a little too passionate for everyday relaxation. I recommend that you maintain the ambient chi energy, but add calming touches. Softer shades of purple with pale yellow accents will do this. Geometric designs, stars or zigzag patterns used, for example, on cushions and curtains or perhaps stencilled on to walls, will support the fire chi energy in this direction.

THE SOUTH-WEST The main feeling here is settled and domestic which is ideal for a cosy relaxed family living room, but it might need sharpening up for social occasions. You could maintain the ambient chi energy but add enhancing touches. Earth colours such as yellow and brown are harmonious, and use purple here and there, perhaps, in a pattern on wallpaper or furnishing fabric. Check patterns will maintain the soil energy here; pointed patterns or shapes, which represent fire chi energy, will enhance it.

THE WEST This is a joyous, pleasurable location, which favours most of the activities likely to take place in a living room, so an appropriate strategy might simply be to maintain this natural ambience. Use soft rusty reds and pinks, with occasional touches of grey and white. Rounded patterns – circles, ovals, stylized flowers, waves or scallops – will add to the favourable metal chi energy of the west. Circular cushions in harmonious colours, or round silver or gold plates hung on the walls would have the same effect.

REMEDIES FOR UNFAVOURABLE LOCATIONS

North and north-east are the least favourable locations for living rooms, being too quiet and too sharp respectively. East and north-west are better, but not ideal, one being too stimulating, the other too formal. These drawbacks can be eased by careful choice of decor and furnishings.

THE NORTH Boost the chi energy here using brighter reds and maroons and by adding metal energy.

THE NORTH-EAST Calm the unsettling chi energy here using sombre reds and more yin surfaces – matt textures, carpets and tapestries.

THE NORTH-WEST Boost the over-serious chi energy here using yellows and browns, and adding soil energy and soft metals such as copper or brass.

THE EAST Calm the over-active chi energy here using more yin pastel greens and more yin materials such as rush matting, and wicker or bamboo furniture.

THE FIREPLACE

Like the sun, a real fire – that is, one that burns coal, wood or gas – is a source of both convected and radiated heat, something which is not true of central heating. A working fireplace can, therefore, greatly enhance the comfortable atmosphere of a home during the winter. This is especially true if you are so far from the Equator that you have limited hours of sunlight. Electric fires, however, are not recommended because they increase electrical radiation (see page 132).

A real fire also provides Five-Element fire chi energy in its pure form, which enhances passion, excitement, spontaneity and brightness. Because of this, it is important, if possible, to position the fireplace in a location where it harmonizes with the Five-Element chi energy in that direction. The more yang warmth of a fire is best suited to the northern part of a building where the usual energy is colder and more yin. On the northern side of the home, the Five-Element chi energy that is most in harmony with fire energy is the soil energy of the north-east. Therefore north-east from the centre of a building or room is the most suitable position for a fireplace.

Of the other positions, east, south-east and south-west are also harmonious in terms of the Five Elements. But being on the more yang sunny side of the home, they are less helpful in other respects. Avoid placing a fire in the south of the building as this could concentrate too much fire energy in one place and increase the risk of a house fire.

Where the fireplace is in a favourable position, you can reflect more fire chi energy back into the room by hanging a mirror above it.

FIRE SUBSTITUTES

In many modern homes it is not possible to have a real fire, but fire chi energy can be introduced in the other forms – lighted candles, lanterns, oil lamps and bright lights, for example. Place them in dark corners where the chi energy is passive. If lights and lamps are impractical, shapes, colours and patterns associated with fire chi energy can be used in the interior decoration. Sharp, pointed or jagged shapes – stars, zigzags, triangles, pyramids – and hot yang colours such as yellows, oranges, reds and purples used in furnishing fabrics or wall coverings will add welcome fire-energy warmth to the room.

Since fire energy is supported by tree energy, tall pointed plants such as palms will also help – especially if they have purple or red flowers – but keep them away from seating areas.

Take care not to overdo these solutions; add one or two items and assess the effects before going further.

Adding fire energy
A tall lamp with a tapering, sharply pleated purple shade and purple or red flowers will help boost fire energy in a room without a fireplace.

83

ARRANGING SEATING AREAS

A living room is likely to be used by several people at a time, so the seating should be arranged to enhance a good sociable atmosphere. Often, if there is an uncomfortable atmosphere in the room, it can be attributed to an unsuccessful arrangement of the chairs and sofas. One general guideline is to have several items of seating (rather than one sofa, for example), and position them so that they all face the centre of the room. This also provides a variety of positions and directions appropriate to the varying needs and desires of your family and friends, and it should be possible for most people to find a direction that suits them (see page 86). Ideally, wherever in the room you are seated, most of the room will be in front of you. This is particularly important for the head of the household.

The positions and directions are most practical when you sit with your back against the wall facing the direction from which you want to benefit. For instance, when facing north is recommended, sit in the south facing the north. This principle applies to your home as a whole

placing sofas and chairs

The harmony of your home can be promoted or obstructed by the way you arrange chairs and sofas. If you place a sofa in the south and two chairs in the north facing it, for example, the chi energies of the north and south will be antagonistic, leading to tension and arguments. Here are examples of more favourable arrangements.

For family harmony
Place a sofa in the north-west facing south-east, with two chairs in front and opposite each other, in the north-east facing south-west and in the south-west facing north-east, and one chair in the south-east facing north-west. Closing the circle of seating in this way makes it particularly harmonious.

as well as to individual rooms. The strongest effects are achieved when you sit in a favourable direction in a room which is itself in the same direction from the centre of your home. If you sit in a the west of a room, which is itself west of the centre of your home, you will strengthen all the effects of the chi energy of the west.

Ideally, arrange seating so that it forms a balanced shape, such as a circle, square or octagon. If necessary, use items like side tables and plants to complete the shapes. Avoid placing chairs or sofas with their backs to windows or doors. In front of a door is the least secure position, especially if people are constantly entering or leaving the room. If possible, place sofas with their backs to the wall.

Make sure, too, that people sitting in chairs are not exposed to cutting chi. For this reason, do not place chairs in front of protruding corners or near sharp-cornered furniture such as coffee tables and sideboards – a solid object such as a sideboard would have a stronger effect than a narrow table top. Also, keep spiky plants away from seating areas. Use bushy plants to absorb cutting chi directed at chairs and sofas.

Avoiding cutting chi
Trail a bushy, round-leaved plant over the sharp corner of a shelf or side table, or cover it with a cloth.

For being productive
Place two sofas opposite each other in the east facing west and the west facing east; and a chair in the north-facing south. This is a dynamic arrangement, good for meetings and getting things done.

For lively conversation
Place two sofas as described left, but in this case place the chair in the north-west facing south-east. This is a more harmonious arrangement where the chair is in balance between the chi energies of the sofas, but is also a lively arrangement good for a social gathering.

where to sit in a room

No matter what room it is, where you sit there can influence your mood, general well-being and your relationships with others. The longer you spend sitting in that place, the stronger the influence will be. The direction you face is slightly more important than the location of your chair from the centre. First decide what you are trying to achieve, or what problem you want to solve. Then use the chart to assess the influences of each direction and decide which one will best suit your needs.

Sitting south facing north
The south places you in fiery radiating chi energy. North is the most peaceful direction, and will help you to feel quieter, more tranquil and meditative.

Sitting south-east facing north-west
The south-east is conducive to communication. Facing north-west is the direction for responsibility and for taking care of your family's needs.

Sitting south-west facing north-east
South-west chi energy is settled and ideal for family harmony. Facing north-east favours motivation, competitiveness and having a sense of purpose. Sit here if you are seeking a new direction in life.

Sitting east facing west
The chi energy in the east is dynamic and busy. Facing west is ideal for romance, pleasure and contentment. This is a good place to relax at the end of the day, and if you want to be close to someone.

Sitting west facing east
The west is conducive to pleasure and romance. Facing east is good for being more active and ambitious. It can help you put your good ideas into practice.

Sitting north-east facing south-west
The north-east enhances motivation. Facing south-west promotes caution, slow methodical progress and practicality. It is helpful if you need to come down to earth, and good for family harmony and deeper relationships.

Sitting north-west facing south-east
This is the leadership position. It places you in a flow of very powerful chi energy. Facing south-east promotes more harmonious progress. It is favourable for communication and creativity – an ideal seat if you want to have a good talk with someone.

Sitting north facing south
The energy of the north is peaceful and calm. Facing south favours being more outgoing and sociable. If you are entertaining friends and you want to be the centre of attention, sit here. It is also good for inspiration and new ideas.

the dining room

Given today's hectic life styles, the evening meal may be the only time of day a family can all be together. However small your home it is important to set aside a special area, even if it can not be an entire room, where you can sit and eat around a table. A successful dining room or dining area creates a pleasant atmosphere where everyone can relax, enjoy their food and take time to digest it properly. It helps, too, if the room is conducive to conversation and family harmony. The food is the focal point; the surroundings have a supporting role.

FOOD AND CHI ENERGY

The food we eat is a major influence on our health. In Oriental medicine food is often an integral part of the treatment. Different foods have their own flow of chi energy. When you eat you take in not only physical nutrients but also the chi energy of the food, which is a vital ingredient in the healing process.

Food's chi energy is easily influenced by the ambient chi energy, so it is essential that the chi energy in a dining room be conducive to good health. Nowadays we all recognise the importance of healthy eating, but we do not always get maximum benefit from our food, not simply because of what we eat, but how we eat it. It is much more healthy to sit down while eating, for example, than to eat on the run. This helps the stomach adopt a shape that is more conducive to proper digestion. Relax and take your time while eating. When you are tense and rushed, you secrete more acids in your stomach, which can lead to indigestion. It also helps to keep conversations at the table positive and enjoyable.

FAVOURABLE LOCATIONS

Ideal positions for the dining room are east, south-east, west and north-west of the centre of your home. East has a more lively atmosphere, and is a particularly good location for breakfasts because the sun shines on the eastern side of your home in the morning. The energy in the south-east favours conversation, and the west contains the chi energy that is best for pleasure, romance and entertainment. It is a particularly good location for the evening meal, because the setting sun naturally energizes this part of your home. The north-west is best for more formal or more serious occasions. Avoid eating north-east from the centre of your home, because the sharp, piercing chi energy there is quick-changing and direct. This is not the right atmosphere for a relaxing meal.

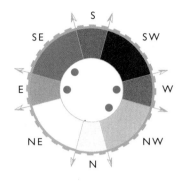

Recommended directions for a dining room
East, south-east, west and north-west of the centre of your home.

EAST *A green and white leaf-patterned fabric maintains tree energy here. Bright greens and blues are harmonious.*

SOUTH-EAST *Dark blues and greens maintain the energy here. Irregular-patterned wallpaper enhances chi energy.*

WEST *Strong dark reds work well in a dining room in this location.*

NORTH-WEST *The dignified chi energy here is maintained by grey and white. Silver table accessories add to metal energy.*

CHOOSING FURNISHINGS

The main aim in a dining area is to maintain the cleanliness required for handling food while promoting the relaxing atmosphere needed for good digestion and a convivial sociable ambience.

FURNITURE Easy-to-clean surfaces are essential. Wood is ideal since it does not speed up chi energy. Different woods affect chi energy differently. Used, for example, in a table, they can alter the ambience of a meal (see opposite). To avoid poor digestion and ill-health, ensure sharp-cornered furniture is not directed at your guests.

LIGHTING Keep it flexible. Low lighting during dinner is romantic, but at other times bright lights are needed. Dimmer switches provide both options. Candles add fire energy, which helps to produce a warm vibrant atmosphere at the dining table.

WINDOW TREATMENTS Fabric roller blinds are preferable to curtains since they avoid stagnation.

FLOOR COVERINGS Natural wood floors have a neutral effect on chi energy and are easy to clean. Avoid rugs and carpets.

PAINTINGS Choose images which provide a sympathetic backdrop to relaxed eating. Still-lifes of food, convivial scenes or restful landscapes are all suitable. An attractive bowl of real fruit on a sideboard would have the same effect.

ACCESSORIES A mirror on the wall or sideboard, reflecting the table, enhances the healthy chi energy produced by the food.

USING COLOUR AND PATTERN

Check the direction of the dining room from the centre of your home. Use background colours and patterns that maintain the chi energy of favourable directions, adding calming or enhancing features to fine-tune chi energy, depending on the ambience you aim to create. If it is a room used throughout the day, use bright colours. Darker shades work best in a dining room used mostly in the evenings.

The east is already vibrant and bright and grassy greens would maintain this. A leaf-patterned wallpaper or fabric with small touches of calming purple would be ideal. In the gentler south-east use more sombre shades of green and blue. An irregular colour-washed finish would be enhancing.

Warm pinks or even a dramatic rusty red could be used on the walls in a western dining room, ideal for evening meals.

To calm chi, colour-wash, rag-roll or sponge the paint on. Soften it further with satin-finish cream paint on the woodwork. The north-west has a certain dignity. Plain painted walls in grey and white with touches of red and silver in accessories, and starched white table linen would enhance this in a formal dining room.

THE DINING TABLE

The shape of the dining table influences the movement of chi energy around it and therefore the atmosphere at meal-times. The shape itself can be more yin or more yang (see right), which itself has an impact. A round or square table is more yang and carries a dynamic chi energy. An oval or rectangular table induces a more gentle energy, which is better for relaxed dining.

Round or oval tables offer the greatest choice of locations for the dining chairs, giving you a better chance of seating your family and guests harmoniously (see page 92). Square and rectangular tables are limited to four directions. If the sides of the table are long and you seat more than two people next to each other, it can be difficult for them to hold a conversation comfortably.

SURFACES

The table top must be easy to clean. Natural wooden surfaces are relatively yielding and easily maintained. Light softwoods such as pine and elm are more yin, and are best for everyday relaxed family meals. Polished dark hardwoods such as oak, mahogany and teak are more yang which is more appropriate for formal occasions such as dinner parties. Hard surfaces like marble and glass speed up the flow of chi energy across the table, making for a more stimulating, more exciting but also more edgy atmosphere, which for some occasions (see right) could be desirable.

The combination of surface with shape allows you to choose the ambience of your dining area. You can combine more yin shapes (rectangles and ovals) with more yang materials and surfaces (marble, granite and glass), and more yang shapes (squares and circles) with more yin materials (light woods), or put yin materials and shapes together and yang materials and shapes together (see right). All these combinations have subtly different effects.

You can also use table linen to adjust the atmosphere of particular meals. Cover more yang surfaces with a large table cloth to slow the energy down. A more yin wooden table might need only a small cloth or place mats. The choice of colours for the table linen will also make an considerable difference (see pages 90–1).

FAVOURABLE TABLES

Different materials and shapes make a table top best suited to some types of occasion rather than others.

Formal dinner parties
A more yin rectangle stretches energy and is more relaxing than a square top. Mahogany is more yang than softwoods, adding formality.

Family meals
An oval top spreads chi energy and is therefore more yin than a round top. A pine surface is also more yin and so particularly relaxing.

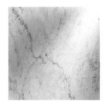

Business lunches
A square top is more yang and stimulating than a rectangular one. A hard marble top is also dynamic.

Romantic suppers
A round table is more yang and therefore more active than an oval one. A glass top adds excitement.

table settings

Your choice of table linen, dishes and accessories has a powerful influence on the ambience around the dining table. Using the concepts of yin and yang (see page 22) you can design quite different settings, which affect the movement of chi energy across the table in a variety of ways.

The table itself is important – its shape and the material it is made of (see page 89). Even minor details, such as a particular plant, a touch of strong bright colour in a table napkin or the shape of a place mat, have subtle effects which contribute to the overall atmosphere in the room.

Choosing appropriate settings for different occasions can make all the difference to the success of a meal, whether it be a formal social event or a casual everyday family affair.

YIN TABLE SETTING

Soft yin surfaces and gentle colours create a more passive flow of chi energy producing a calmer, more relaxed ambience suitable for informal lunches or suppers and for easy-going everyday family meals.

TABLE TOP *Elongated ovals are more yin than compact round or square shapes. The light wooden surface has a neutral effect on the movement of chi energy.*

CHAIR *Pale unvarnished softwoods such as pine or elm and fabric coverings or upholstery made from natural fibres like linen and cotton are more yin.*

PLACE MAT *Cork, linen, wicker, bamboo or rush place mats have a calming effect.*

TABLE LINEN *Neutral colours and natural fibres are more yin. The cloth itself slows the movement of chi.*

CUTLERY AND CHOPSTICKS *Wood-handled cutlery and wooden chopsticks create a lighter, more relaxed, more yin atmosphere.*

NAPKIN *Green symbolizes living plants. Dark or sombre shades of green enhance communication.*

PLATES *Wooden bowls and platters, and rough-textured earthenware and stoneware are all more yin.*

PLANT *Bushy plants with rounded leaves are calming. Bright green adds vitality.*

FOOD *Watery cooling foods such as salads and fruit are more yin.*

ENHANCING A MOOD WITH COLOUR

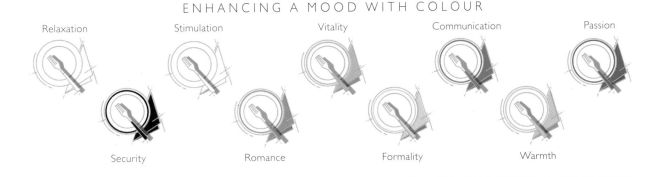

Relaxation   Stimulation   Vitality   Communication   Passion

Security   Romance   Formality   Warmth

YANG TABLE SETTING

This is exciting, stimulating and better suited to formal occasions. With the right touches, however, it can take on a romantic note. Yang settings are spare and ordered with clean lines, strong colours and hard surfaces.

TABLE TOP *Hard shiny materials such as marble encourage a faster flow of chi energy. The compact square shape is also more yang. Square mats have a similar effect.*

CHAIR *Shiny bare metal furniture is generally more yang and encourages a faster more dynamic flow of chi energy. A cushion in yang red or orange would intensify the effect.*

CUTLERY AND GLASS *Reflective surfaces of polished metal cutlery and sparkling glasses spin chi energy around the table making for a more stimulating yang atmosphere.*

CANDLES *These add fire energy and passion.*

ROSES *Red roses symbolize passionate love, giving a romantic emphasis to this yang setting.*

FOOD *Bread made from wholegrain flour is more yang than bread made, from white flour. Salmon is a strong yang fish that swims upstream. The smoking process makes it even more yang.*

TABLE LINEN *Touches of red in the napkins and the candle add a dynamic element to the setting.*

where to sit around a table

A favourable seating plan creates a harmonious atmosphere at the dining table. Each location is linked with a typical family member who represents the kind of chi energy located there. The chi energy may not be literally that of the person involved, but he or she is likely to feel more comfortable there.

The plan below provides an insight into the nature of chi energy around the table. Use it to evaluate the possible effects on the diners. This plan assumes a round table. A rectangular or square one may need to be angled so that people can sit in the most suitable places. Do not seat them opposite corners.

Sitting south facing north
This seat brings out the expressive, passionate side of people. It is traditionally linked with the middle daughter or a middle-aged woman. Facing north is quiet and mysterious.

Sitting south-east facing north-west
Because it promotes communication, this location is good for someone you want to be more talkative. Represented by the eldest daughter, it favours young women generally. Facing north-west adds dignity and respect.

Sitting south-west facing north-east
Associated with the mother, this place is conducive to family harmony. Facing north-east is motivating and leads to hard work.

Sitting east facing west
This is a good place for feeling more active and ambitious – ideal for a young man. Traditionally, it is the seat of the eldest son. Facing west adds romance and contentment.

Sitting west facing east
This seat enhances romance and pleasure. The chi energy here is both playful and teasing which is good for a young girl, so it is linked with the youngest daughter. Facing east favours being busy and confident.

Sitting north-east facing south-west
Motivation is enhanced in this position, so the youngest son does well here. For others it is not particularly good, especially on a regular basis.

Sitting north-west facing south-east
Beneficial for leadership, this is traditionally the father's seat. It is authoritative and commands respect. Facing south-east favours communication and harmony.

Sitting north facing south
It is quiet and still here, but facing south is full of passion and excitement – suitable for a middle son or middle-aged man.

the bedroom

We spend on average six to nine hours out of every twenty-four in bed. For most of us, this is the longest time in a day that we are in one place, so the location and design of the bedroom and the positioning of the bed provide a superb opportunity to align yourself with the natural flow of energy in a way that helps you in other areas of your life.

A good night's sleep is essential for health, so it is also important to have a bedroom that calms you at the end of a busy day, and helps you to sleep well. It should also be a place where you wake up feeling refreshed, full of vitality and enthusiasm to make the most of a new day.

The bedroom has a significant influence on adult relationships, being where sex and physical intimacy take place. If you live in a large family, your bedroom is often the only place that is exclusively yours, and privacy is also an important consideration. If possible, it is better not to use your bedroom for activities that require a different atmosphere, such as work. In the end, both will suffer.

FAVOURABLE LOCATIONS

Sometimes people have their beds in locations and directions that make their lives in general, not just sleep and sex, more difficult. Ideally, your bedroom should be exposed to sunlight at dawn which helps to increase your energy in the morning. If you have a choice of rooms, choose one where the atmosphere is calmest. The ideal direction for your bed is determined by what you are trying to achieve (see pages 102–3).

The most favourable positions for the bedroom of an adult or older person are north-west, north and west of the centre of your home. The north-west is ideal for parents. The chi energy here is more mature and can lead to greater responsibility, respect from others and improved ability to organize your life. The north has a quieter, more peaceful chi energy. This is particularly helpful for anyone who has difficulty sleeping. Young people, however, should avoid sleeping with their heads pointing north as this could make their whole lives too quiet. West is particularly favourable for romance, pleasure and contentment – desirable qualities in a bedroom shared by a couple. If your sex life has become dull, moving your bedroom to the north or west may bring increased or more satisfying sexual activity.

Generally, younger people benefit from a bedroom in the east or south-east of the home since they are building up their lives and the chi energy there favours making a good start.

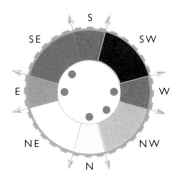

***Recommended directions
for a bedroom***
*North, east, south-east, west and
north-west of the centre of your home.*

an ideal bedroom

The chi energy of the west favours romance and contentment, making it an ideal location for a master bedroom. This position fulfils the principal requirements of promoting relaxation, restful sleep and the quiet privacy necessary to foster intimate relationships. But the room should also contain lively, uplifting, cheerful elements to make it a pleasant place in which to wake up and begin the day. There is a playful aspect to the chi energy of the west which will produce this effect.

❶ LIGHTING *Soft yin lighting is restful and intimate. Lampshades diffuse the harshness of electric light. Candles provide a more natural romantic glow and, if placed in the north-east, they support soil energy.*

❷ PLANTS *Round-leaved plants are soothing and, in the west or north-west of the room, help to maintain metal energy.*

❸ STORAGE *Have plenty of cupboard and wardrobe space, and keep clothes and possessions tucked away. Cupboards in alcoves or across an entire wall help reduce cutting chi.*

❹ BED *A wood-framed bed has a neutral effect on chi energy. A headboard protects your head from a fast flow of energy, though if your bed is against a wall this is less important.*

Place your bed in a favourable direction (see page 98). Sleeping with your head pointing north-west enhances the chi energy of leadership, organization and responsibility – good for parents. Wherever you sleep, you should be able to see the door and windows from your bed.

❺ BED LINEN *To create a harmonious flow of chi energy next to your skin, use bed linen made of cotton, linen or silk. Shades of pink and circular patterns support the chi energy of the west. Do not leave beds unmade during the day.*

❻ FURNITURE *Bedroom furniture should have round edges. Sharp corners should not face the bed. Cutting chi directed at you while you sleep will disturb your chi energy and could affect your health.*

❼ FLOOR COVERING *Soft yin materials slow chi energy and create a relaxing atmosphere, so a fitted carpet is ideal in a bedroom.*

❽ WINDOW TREATMENT *Full draped or ruched curtains slow the flow of chi energy through the windows at night and so promote restful sleep. Keep them tightly closed while you sleep, especially if the window is open.*

❾ WALL COVERING *Pastel colours are more yin and calming. Pink is harmonious in west locations.*

❿ PAINTINGS *Avoid reflective yang surfaces in bedrooms; tapestries or pictures with no or non-reflecting glass are appropriate. Placing objects such as pictures, candles and table lamps in pairs symbolizes intimacy.*

Five-Element remedies
To enhance the metal energy of the west and increase the romantic ambience, place a vase of red flowers in the west of the room.

THINGS TO AVOID IN A BEDROOM

SHARP CORNERS Because of the length of time you spend sleeping, it is especially important to avoid cutting chi in bedrooms, especially if it is directed at the bed. Avoid spiky plants and square or rectangular furniture near the bed.
MIRRORS These reflect your own chi back at you while you sleep and impede the process of getting rid of old emotions. Do not have them at all in bedrooms, or cover or turn them to the wall at night.

YANG MATERIALS Hard shiny surfaces like glass, metal and marble speed up chi energy and could prevent you getting a good night's sleep.
EN SUITE BATHROOMS These are undesirable because bathrooms introduce a heavier, damper atmosphere into bedrooms, and may drain them of healthy chi. Keep the door to an en suite bathroom closed, or screen the entrance with a curtain.

A bedroom in the west
The west is characterized by metal energy,
which is maintained here with
more yin calming
touches.

CHOOSING THE DECOR

In a western room the decor should support the metal chi energy there, which is favourable for a bedroom. Maintain it using pinks, white and grey, and increase it with touches of red, silver and gold. More red increases the romantic ambience, and more yin pastel shades, or off-white or cream, creates peace and tranquillity. Rounded patterns on fabrics and wallpaper also maintain metal energy. Irregular patterns produced by sponging and colour-washing are calming if you have trouble sleeping.

NORTH *Warm pink, burgundy or red will increase vitality in an otherwise quiet and reflective northern bedroom.*

NORTH-WEST *Grey, white and pink will maintain the natural sombre energy in this location.*

EAST AND SOUTH-EAST *Blues and greens will help to maintain active tree energy in both these locations.*

DECOR FOR OTHER FAVOURABLE LOCATIONS

THE NORTH The chi energy here is particularly quiet and tranquil. It fosters introspection and spirituality and, while it favours older people and anyone suffering from insomnia, it is not so favourable for young people. Depending on your situation, you may wish to maintain the naturally cool chi energy using cream and off-white, or perhaps enhance it with warmer pinks and reds.

THE NORTH-WEST The natural ambience here is responsible and serious, but again, perhaps too sombre for younger people. To maintain it, use grey, white and pink. Check patterns which incorporate some yellow, brown or black would add soil energy to support the metal energy here.

EAST AND SOUTH-EAST Both these locations are better for younger people since they are generally stimulating and lively, especially in the mornings where they are exposed to the rising sun. Use more yin middle or pastel shades of green or blue and irregular patterns to calm the atmosphere for sleeping.

REMEDIES FOR UNFAVOURABLE LOCATIONS

South and north-east are the least favourable locations for a bedroom. The former is too hot and fiery to encourage healthy sleep; the latter is too unpredictable and sharp and could lead to the people sleeping there having nightmares. Both locations need calming. The south-west is also undesirable, but in this case the chi energy would produce too sluggish an influence on your daily life, and yet it is also unstable. It needs both stabilizing and stimulating.

THE NORTH-EAST Calm the sharp, piercing chi energy here using pale yellows or rusty colours rather than bright shades of red and pink. Add helpful metal energy with more yin curved, rather than more yang circular, patterns or objects.

THE SOUTH Calm the excessively passionate chi energy in this location using pale yin shades of purple and the soil colours yellow and black. Soft matt textures, such as those on carpets, tapestries and upholstered furniture, will also help. Add soil energy using check patterns, low spreading plants in unglazed terracotta pots or unglazed clay sculptures.

THE SOUTH-WEST Stimulate the settled chi energy here using bright yellows and browns with touches of rich purple. Adding metal energy in its more yin forms – bronze and copper – will provide more stability.

THE BED

Most people think of the bed only as a place to sleep and engage in sexual intimacy, but the right bed can also revitalize your energy, influence aspects of your everyday life and, indeed, shape your destiny.

Wood is the most favourable material for the bed frame. Unlike metal, it does not alter the local magnetic field and has a more subtle influence on the movement of chi energy. Metal bed frames, such as brass and cast iron, speed up chi energy, which is not generally conducive to sound and restful sleep. Water beds are not recommended as they produce a damp heavy atmosphere, leading to stagnation.

A headboard will protect your head from fast-flowing chi while you sleep, but is less important if your bedhead is placed against a wall.

Keep the space beneath your bed empty to avoid chi energy stagnating under you while you sleep. If you store things under your bed, clear it out and clean there regularly

THE MATTRESS

Choose a mattress made of natural materials. Cotton, wool, straw and hair are preferable to foam and other synthetics, which carry a static charge that can make you feel drained of physical and emotional energy. Pocket-sprung mattresses contain metal springs which affect the local magnetic field and cause the movement of chi energy to become chaotic. This can make people sleeping on them feel confused and disorientated.

Futons are ideal beds in Feng Shui terms. They are made of four to eight layers of thick cotton wadding bound by a strong cotton cover. In Japan they place them on the floor on bamboo tatami mats, but in the West most people use wooden bases to raise them off the floor so that they can air properly.

BED LINEN

Since they are used next to your skin, it is even more important that sheets, pillowcases, blankets and duvet covers are made of pure cotton, linen, silk or wool. Cotton and linen are preferable because they "breathe" better than silk. Avoid synthetic fabrics. Quilts and duvets, likewise, should contain only natural down or cotton filling. Keep bed linen and bedcovers raised well above the floor, so that air can circulate freely under the bed. All bedding should be regularly washed and also well aired, preferably outside.

Choose colours of bed linen to harmonize with the Eight Directions (see page 123). An alternative approach would be to match them to your own personal Nine Ki colours (see page 37).

ENHANCING ROMANCE

▼

The romantic atmosphere in a bedroom can be enhanced in several ways.

COLOURS Careful use of red and purple – the colours of romance and passion – can be effective. Try a vase of red flowers or a wall-hanging with purple touches. For maximum effect, place something purple to the south of the room and something red to the west.

OBJECTS When choosing decorative objects for the bedroom, think about their psychological effects. If you find images that inspire passionate and loving feelings in you, they may also do so in your partner.

PAIRS Keeping objects in pairs helps to reinforce close relationships. This could be a pair of paintings or sculptures, two plants in the same pot or a pair of candlesticks.

CANDLES These increase the fire energy associated with passion, but extinguish them before you go to sleep.

directions for the bed

The choice of rooms may be limited, but the position of the bed itself is often more flexible. The direction you sleep in affects your whole life as well as how well you sleep. Ideally, place the bed along an axis that passes through the centre of the home, and so that your head will point in a helpful direction.

	Head pointing **NORTH**	This quiet direction can help with insomnia, but it can also make your whole life too quiet. Some Feng Shui masters refer to it as the death position as it is beneficial for people in their later years. It enhances feelings of peace, tranquillity and spirituality.
	Head pointing **NORTH-EAST**	This direction is too sharp and piercing for good sleep. It can make you feel on edge and increase violent nightmares. It may improve your motivation but it is inadvisable to sleep like this over a long period.
	Head pointing **EAST**	This is ideal for young people. It makes you feel that everything is before you, that tomorrow is a new day and anything can happen. Good for career-building, ambition and getting things done, it is ideal for growth and for making life busier.
	Head pointing **SOUTH-EAST**	Good communication and increased creativity are the benefits you can expect from sleeping in this direction. It will encourage growth and a more active life, but in a more subtle way than the east.
	Head pointing **SOUTH**	Its high energy and hot fiery nature means this direction is not conducive to sound sleep. It can also lead to heated arguments with the possible risk of separation. While it enhances the passion in your life, use it only in the short term.
	Head pointing **SOUTH-WEST**	This is a settled position which implies more peaceful relationships, but it can make you too cautious. It also means you will now be sleeping with your feet pointing north-east. The north-east/south-west axis can make your life more unstable.
	Head pointing **WEST**	This combines a good sleep with a general atmosphere of contentment, and may even improve income and romance. But the feelings of contentment can also lead to laziness and low motivation, so west is more suited to those already established in their careers.
	Head pointing **NORTH-WEST**	This is associated with leadership and feeling in control of things, and promotes longer deeper sleep. It is best suited to for someone older who has the experience to exercise authority wisely, and is recommended for parents.

the children's room

This often has to function as a bedroom and playroom, so the challenge is to make it fun during the day and peaceful at night. Balancing these two considerations will affect your choice of location, the direction in which you place the bed or beds, and furnishing and decor. For many parents the ideal children's bedroom is one where they sleep soundly the whole night through, but the chi energy in the room must also be supportive of the needs of growing children for activity and stimulation.

Sometimes two or more children may have to share a room and this can lead to friction. If you place all the beds in the same direction, it can make relations between the children more harmonious. If your own relationship with a particular child is strained, place your bed and the child's bed in the same direction at least for a short time or until the problems have eased.

If several children share a room, make sure they each have a space, however small, they can call their own. It could be a shelf, drawer, storage unit or their own small desk or table. Allow them to organize these spaces themselves and resist the temptation to interfere.

FAVOURABLE LOCATIONS

Ideally, your children's bedroom should be exposed to energizing sunlight at dawn. This would be the case in the east and south-east of your home. The west, which receives sun in the afternoon, is also favourable, especially for children who tend to be hyperactive.

The east contains the youthful uplifting chi energy associated with growing and developing. The chi energy there is stimulating and active, and represents the rising sun, which symbolizes the future. It has the feeling of the beginning of a new day, just as a child is at the beginning of a new life. Achieving restful sleep could be a problem, however, as the chi energy in the east may be too active, and you may need to take steps to calm it (see pages 100–1).

A bedroom in the south-east can also promote growth and lively activity. But the chi energy here is gentler than in the east, and could encourage a more harmonious development in life. It is also a more soothing place for sleeping.

The west carries a more settled chi energy and would be the best location for a peaceful night's sleep. The chi energy here is playful, but does not convey the same benefits as the other directions in terms of the child's harmonious growth and development.

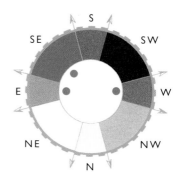

Recommended directions for a children's room
East, south-east, and west of the centre of your home.

an ideal child's room

The chi energy of the east is ideal for a growing child, being bright, positive, forward-looking and active. It supports one of the main functions of children's rooms – to encourage imaginative play and stimulate the child's healthy mental development.

At the same time, sound rest is vital for a child, so the liveliness of the east may need to be moderated. Balance the need for stimulation with the room's other main purpose – providing a calm peaceful environment which promotes sound sleep.

1 LIGHTING *Uplights reflecting off the ceiling support tree energy. To avoid trailing flexes, use wall lights instead of table or floor lamps.*

2 STORAGE *Plenty of units keep the room clear for play. Place within reach so children can put away their own toys. Floor boxes are ideal.*

3 BEDS *Bunk beds save space and also allow you to place two children in the same sleeping direction – helpful if they squabble. If your baby is not sleeping, place the cot so that the baby's head is pointing north. The beds should be cosy and inviting. Have plump pillows and fluffy duvets in natural fibres. Blue is a harmonious colour in this direction.*

4 FURNITURE *Rounded stools and tables reduce the risk of cutting chi. Children face east when they sit at the table in the east of the room, intensifying the active chi energy here. Bright colours are stimulating.*

5 FLOOR COVERING *Natural wood supports tree energy, reduces stagnation and is easy to clean.*

6 WINDOW TREATMENT *Fabric blinds slow chi energy through the window at night, without risking stagnation. When rolled up in the day, they uncover the window completely, maximizing the room's exposure to favourable chi.*

7 WALL COVERING *Softer, shades of blue are harmonious and calming. Stars adds fire energy.*

8 PAINTINGS *Fabric wall-hangings slow chi energy and are not reflective (see below). Choose positive images to suit your children's needs. Bright colours, particularly red, yellow and orange, are more yang and therefore stimulating. Soft colours, particularly blues and greens, are more yin and soothing.*

9 MOBILE *The gentle movement of mobiles can be arousing or relaxing for a young child. Place a more yang, shiny metal mobile in the west of the room. For a stronger effect, paint it in bright primary colours. A soft fabric mobile in pastel colours would be more yin and peaceful. Do not hang mobiles directly over a child's bed.*

10 TOYS *Wood is ideal for toys because it is a natural material as well as being strong and durable, yet warm and pleasing to touch. Put toys away at night to calm chi energy.*

Five-Element remedy *If children are frightened or wary of the dark, place a natural flame night light in a safe holder in the room rather than add to electrical radiation. Fire energy is calming in an east room. The fire chi of a starry purple holder also helps.*

THINGS TO AVOID IN CHILDREN'S ROOMS

OPEN DOORS Keep the bedroom door closed at night and draw the curtains. This will calm the flow of energy so that the children fall asleep easily.
BEDHEADS BELOW WINDOWS Do not place bedheads under windows as the chi energy here is more active and may prevent a good night's sleep.
HEAVY FURNITURE Children need space, and bulky furniture can make the room feel obstructive and confining.

CLUTTER It is easy for children's rooms to become littered with their toys and possessions, ultimately becoming confusing and frustrating. Encourage them to keep the room tidy and to get rid of outgrown items.
ELECTRICAL EQUIPMENT To reduce unnecessary electrical radiation, do not have TVs, video machines and personal computers in children's bedrooms.

A children's room in the east
*The decor here is chosen to support
the tree energy of the east but also
add calming touches.*

INTERNAL DOOR

CHOOSING THE DECOR

Maintain the favourable active tree chi energy here using
harmonious blue as a background colour but in softer, more
yin shades to introduce a calmer note. Elsewhere in the room,
bright greens, yellows and blues in smaller quantities will also
be harmonious, yet stimulating. Plain walls and bed covers are more
yang, and will help to reduce any impression of clutter from playthings
and toys. Yellow is harmonious in any direction. Star motifs introduce
fire energy and are calming to the tree energy of the east. To calm it
more, use very soft yin pastel shades and bring in more pale purple.

SLEEPING DIRECTIONS

▼

Similar considerations apply to the location of children's beds as to adults' (see page 98), but you can also use Feng Shui principles to solve problems that apply especially to children. The directions referred to below apply to the head of the bed.

East or south-east are generally the most favourable positions, though the east may be too active for children with sleeping problems.

West and north are helpful for children who cannot sleep, and the north is especially suitable for newborn babies.

The following directions are undesirable: the north-east is too harsh and could cause tantrums; the south is too fiery and could be disturbing; the south-west is too mature and could lead to timidity; the north-west is too serious – the child may eventually try to control its parents.

SOUTH-EAST *Vertically striped patterns of harmonious green and blue will maintain the buoyant energy of a room in this location.*

DECOR FOR OTHER FAVOURABLE LOCATIONS

THE SOUTH-EAST   This location shares many characteristics with the east (see page 100–1), but is gentler so it will not be necessary to introduce so many calming devices into a children's room here. Maintaining the natural ambience should be sufficient. Use stronger shades of the harmonious colours – greens and blues – while keeping them bright and cheerful, rather than sombre. Patterns with a vertical motif would also be appropriate here.

THE WEST   This has a settled, contented feeling which could well suit an anxious or overactive child, or where children are going through a squabbling phase. But if you need to introduce a more stimulating, energizing quality to the room, use yang shades of red and pink, together with touches of bright yellow. Check patterns will also help.

REMEDIES FOR UNFAVOURABLE LOCATIONS

The problems which make north-east, south, south-west and and north-west unsuitable directions for children to sleep in (see left), apply equally to them as locations for the room as a whole. The north could be used on a temporary basis, but would not be a good long-term position.

THE NORTH Boost the quiet chi energy here by adding yang metal energy: bright reds, shiny metal mobiles and metal wind chimes would all help.

THE NORTH-EAST Calm the sharp chi energy here with more yin soil and metal energies: rusty pinks, pale yellow and generous use of fabrics and other soft matt surfaces.

Place a cloth mobile in a harmonious colour, in the north-east of the room.

THE SOUTH Calm the hyperactive chi energy here with more yin soil energy, as in the north-east, but use pale yellow and buff rather than pink and place a terracotta bowl containing charcoal under the bed.

THE SOUTH-WEST Boost the over-mature chi by adding more yang fire and metal energies: purples, reds and pinks in zigzag or circular patterns.

THE NORTH-WEST Calm the over-solemn chi energy here by adding water chi energy: creamy colours and irregularly patterned walls.

WEST *The metal energy of this direction can be enhanced with yang shades of red, pink and bright yellow in check patterns.*

the kitchen

Food has special significance in the Far East because it is widely used for healing. Practitioners of Oriental medicine believe that a healthy well-balanced diet leads to good health and longevity. Yin and yang and the Five Elements can be applied to food as they can to a building, and part of a traditional Oriental physician's job is to advise on a patient's diet in accordance with these principles.

Air, water and food provide not only life-sustaining nutrients, but also each has its own flow of chi energy. There is relatively little we can do about the air we breathe, but we have more choice about drinking water and a much greater choice over the food we eat and how it is prepared. How we exercise those choices has a direct influence on our health and well-being.

Food preparation is influenced by the surrounding chi energy, so the siting of the kitchen in a favourable location is vital. Since kitchens combine the incompatible elements of fire and water, the location must be one where these elements can be harmonized, and particular consideration must be given to positioning the stove and sink (see page 106). Facing a helpful direction while you are cooking can also help you prepare more interesting, healthier meals (see page 105).

FAVOURABLE LOCATIONS

The most suitable positions are to the east and south-east of the centre of your home, where the energy is bright, uplifting and supportive to growth, activity and development. Also, the Five-Element tree energy of the east and south-east is compatible with both water and fire. The resulting harmonious flow of energy through the kitchen will benefit the movement of chi energy throughout the home. The early morning sun warms and energizes the east and south-east sides of the home, which makes them particularly good locations for kitchens which double as breakfast rooms.

Certain locations should be avoided if at all possible. The north-east, where the chi energy is cold, piercing and quick-changing, is not the best atmosphere for creating healthy well-balanced meals. The north, being quiet and still, does not have sufficient vitality to promote good health. A kitchen in the south is also particularly undesirable since it would be in the position of Five-Element fire energy, thus concentrating too much fire energy in one place, which is likely to produce unbalanced meals and increase the risk of house fires.

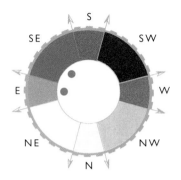

Recommended directions for a kitchen
East and south-east of the centre of your home.

CHOOSING FURNISHINGS

The kitchen should be bright, clean and dry, which will have a positive influence on the chi energy of your food before you eat it.

PLANTS   Place healthy leafy plants between the stove and sink to harmonize fire and water.

LIGHTING   Dark corners are harder to keep clean and risk stagnation. Natural light is ideal; complement it with spotlights directed at the corners. Encourage sunlight into the room to create an uplifting atmosphere. Sunlight also helps keep the kitchen dry, and therefore the chi energy fresh and clean. If the room is dark have a fireplace or wood-burning stove.

FOOD AND FLOWERS   Bowls of fruit and other displays of fresh foods and flowers promote a healthy flow of chi energy.

FURNITURE   Wood is the ideal surface for food preparation. Stainless steel and shiny ceramic tiles create a more yang, fast-moving atmosphere, but this may become a problem if you spend a good deal of time in the kitchen. Laminates and vinyl tiles tend to block chi energy. Fit cupboards, shelves and worktops with rounded corners and edges to avoid cutting chi.

FLOORS   Natural wood flooring is recommended, being practical, warm and easy to clean. Cork tiles are the most yin wooden flooring material. Avoid carpets and rugs.

STORAGE   Do not allow the room to become cluttered with appliances, gadgets and utensils, which causes stagnation resulting in harmful influences on food preparation. Have well-arranged storage space and keep surfaces clean and tidy. Wash down open shelves and clear out cupboards regularly.

FRESH AIR   To keep chi energy moving and remove humidity, open the windows each day. This is preferable to extractors which stir up chi.

PLUMBING   Keep taps in good repair and sinks unblocked.

USING COLOUR AND PATTERN

Enhance the favourable chi energy in an eastern or south-eastern kitchen using off-white or cream as the main colours, with bright green in the east and dark greens and blues in the south-east used as accents. The chi energy in these locations will be boosted by irregular patterns, whether in decorative paint finishes on walls and woodwork, or in a wallpaper or fabric with a figurative motif. An all-over leaf pattern would maintain tree energy here; or choose a culinary theme such as vegetables or fruits. Watery subjects in harmonious blues would also be appropriate because Five-Element water energy is supportive to tree energy.

MATERIALS *Shiny ceramic tiles help keep chi energy moving and prevent stagnation. Cork flooring is more yin, enabling you to spend lots of time comfortably in the kitchen.*

COLOURS *Blues and greens maintain tree energy in the east and south-east. Touches of purple are enhancing and yellow is harmonious in any direction.*

MOTIFS *Images of fruit and vegetables in harmonious colours are sympathetic in a kitchen.*

THE STOVE

In Feng Shui, the stove represents the creation of life, because the food prepared on it contributes to the creation of life in your body. It is the most important appliance in the kitchen, and should be as large as space permits. If your stove is positioned against a wall, hang a mirror on the wall above it. This will visually double its size, thus enhancing the life-creating image. You will also be able to see what is happening behind you when you are cooking.

Stoves with a natural flame are preferable. Gas is ideal, but wood- or coal-burning stoves are good alternatives. A natural flame stove, like a real fire, also adds to the comfortable atmosphere of the room. Avoid electric stoves, since these give off electromagnetic fields, which can negatively affect the chi energy of your food, and consequently your health. Microwaves are also not recommended (see page 132). Surfaces must be easy to clean; stainless steel is the best choice for a stove top.

A helpful position for the stove is on an island in the kitchen, as this will allow you to face into the room while you are cooking and to see the windows and doors. It also gives you a greater choice of positions within the kitchen, so that you can face the direction most favourable to you (see below). Facing into the room also makes for a more sociable setting, enabling you feel less isolated and to see and talk to your friends and family while you are cooking for them.

COOKING POSITIONS

The direction you face while cooking has an influence on the meals you create. Facing north is the least helpful direction since its quiet chi energy is not conducive to the busy atmosphere needed for preparing meals. Facing west is settling and could be helpful for someone who was too perfectionist and obsessive about cooking, but for others it could lead to laziness.

People who enjoy complicated recipes will find facing the south-west helps them to be methodical and practical. On the other hand, if you tend to be over-competitive, avoid the north-east, which will accentuate these tendencies. It is also a volatile direction so you would be likely to rush the preparation of your dish, and ruin it as a result. Facing south will increase your enthusiasm for cooking, ideal for preparing quick exciting meals, but it can also be too stimulating and not so good for spending a long time at the stove.

Facing east or south-east are both generally favourable directions. The east is good for being busy, active and practical, and the south-east could lead to you being more creative with your cooking. It is also favourable for feeling organized and in control of the kitchen.

Adding metal and soil energies
The effects of kitchens located in unfavourable positions (see page 106) can be eased by adding soil energy or metal energy. Using clay pots or stainless steel pans would be appropriate means of doing this.

positioning the stove and sink

The stove and sink represent fire and water Five-Element chi energy respectively and should be carefully positioned to avoid disharmony. Ideally, do not place them next to each other. If possible, also keep other water elements, such as refrigerators, dishwashers and washing machines, away from the stove, although this is less important. Try to ensure the stove and sink are in helpful locations in the kitchen, and ones where the Five-Element chi energy is compatible (see below). On your floor plan place the grid of the Eight Directions over the kitchen to determine the directions of the possible locations and position them accordingly.

If existing installations are in unfavourable positions and cannot be moved, use Five-Element remedies to mitigate the consequences.

DIRECTION	EFFECTS	SOLUTION
NORTH unfavourable	The chi energy here is too quiet to promote health and vitality.	Add more metal chi energy. Stainless steel surfaces, saucepans and other objects that are round or made of metal will help. Red, white and silver are helpful colours.
NORTH-EAST unfavourable	This direction is on an unstable axis, making it too unpredictable and disorientating.	To stabilize chi energy, place small china bowls filled with sea salt in the south-west and north-east corners.
EAST favourable	Fire and water mix harmoniously with the tree chi energy of the east, so this location is beneficial for both stove and sink. The chi energy here is active and helpful in avoiding the risk of stagnation in damp areas.	
SOUTH-EAST favourable	The tree chi energy here is harmonious with fire and water chi energies. Although not as active as in the east, it is enough to avoid stagnation.	
SOUTH unfavourable	The fire chi energy here makes this unfavourable for the stove, because too much fire energy would be concentrated in one place, increasing the risk of accidental fires.	Add more soil energy: low, flat things made of clay or charcoal in a low clay pot. Black and yellow are helpful colours.
SOUTH-WEST unfavourable	This direction is on an unstable axis, making it too unpredictable and disorientating.	To stabilize chi energy, place small china bowls filled with sea salt in the south-west and north-east corners.
WEST unfavourable	In this direction metal energy clashes with the fire energy of the stove, and is drained by the water energy of the sink.	Add more soil energy (charcoal in a low clay pot) near the stove, and metal energy (white flowers in a metal pot) next to the sink.
NORTH-WEST unfavourable	In this direction metal energy clashes with the fire energy of the stove, and is drained by the water energy of the sink.	Add more soil energy (charcoal in a low clay pot) near the stove, and metal energy (white flowers in a metal pot) next to the sink.

the bathroom

Water is the main element in the bathroom. Rooms with a lot of water tend to have damp wet surfaces and more humid atmospheres than other rooms. This can lead to a heavier flow of chi energy, which makes it prone to stagnation. The situation is particularly risky when there is little or no exposure to sunlight and fresh air, so internal bathrooms without windows are the least desirable. Bathrooms are often tucked away in small spaces in a home, but large bathrooms are preferable since it is easier to avoid a harmful build-up of damp stagnant chi energy if there is plenty of space.

Although it is increasingly fashionable to have en suite bathrooms, linked to bedrooms, these are undesirable in Feng Shui terms and should be avoided (see also page 94).

The toilet is often located in the bathroom, which compounds all the problems associated with these rooms, because the draining downward influence of the toilet is especially damaging (see page 109).

FAVOURABLE LOCATIONS

The activities which take place in bathrooms all involve Five-Element water chi energy in its pure form, so it is important to locate them carefully. Another consideration is the draining effect of the bath, shower and toilet, making it difficult to locate bathrooms in positions that are helpful to the flow of chi energy in the home generally. If they are in unfavourable locations, this can have a harmful draining effect on chi energy in the rest of the home. Whatever the direction, it is best not to locate the bathroom opposite the main door, near staircases or near the dining room or kitchen.

The most favourable positions for the bathroom and toilet are east and south-east of the centre of your home. Water is supportive to the Five-Element tree chi energy of the east and south-east and, as long as there are plenty of windows, this is also often a sunny part of the house, which will help to keep the room dry. The dryness and the exposure to sunlight are also both helpful in preventing stagnation.

The least desirable location is in the north-east of your home, which should be avoided if at all possible, and the other locations all risk varying consequences for your physical and mental health. In many homes, however, the position of the bathroom is fixed and there is nothing you can practically do about it. Use Five-Element solutions to mitigate the negative effects (see pages 110).

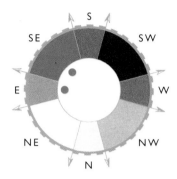

Recommended directions for a bathroom
East and south-east of the centre of your home.

COLOURS *Green and blue used in bathroom accessories support tree energy in the east and south-east.*

MATERIALS *Hard, smooth and preferably reflective materials used on floors, walls and other surfaces speed up the flow of chi energy, which helps reduce the risk of stagnation in humid bathrooms.*

CHOOSING FURNISHINGS

The main objectives in a bathroom are to keep the room bright, dry and fresh and to counteract the tendency for chi energy to stagnate in humid conditions.

LIGHTING Natural light is best. A bright sunny room creates a lively dry atmosphere and sunlight charges up the chi energy of the room and helps stimulate its flow. If natural light is limited, keep the room well lit, especially the corners. Bright lights stimulate chi energy.

FRESH AIR Good ventilation dispels humidity and helps to prevent stagnation. Open the window and let in plenty of fresh air every day. This is preferable to using electric extracator fans.

WINDOW TREATMENTS Slatted blinds are a good compromise between the needs of privacy and those of light. Avoid thick curtains. Keep blinds or curtains open as much as possible.

PLANTS Plenty of leafy plants make the room feel fresh and alive and minimize the risk of chi energy stagnating in corners. Plants also help to absorb the extra humidity in steamy bathrooms, and generally grow well there for that reason.

FURNITURE Keep furniture and bric-a-brac to a minimum. Too many objects in the bathroom create a damper, more stagnant atmosphere. Avoid overuse of fabrics, in particular. Surfaces should be easy to keep clean and dry. Hard shiny surfaces such as chrome, glazed ceramic tiles, polished marble and glass are more yang and stimulate the flow of chi energy, counteracting stagnation.

MIRRORS Mirrors speed up the flow of chi energy, which is a positive feature in a bathroom where you are striving to avoid stagnation. Since bathrooms are often small, mirrors can also give a feeling of space. But do not have mirrors facing each other (see page 148).

USING COLOUR AND PATTERN

Enhance the vibrant chi energy in favourable east and south-east locations using mainly cream and off-white in the paintwork and bathroom fittings. Use bright green in the east and dark blues and greens in the south-east in accessories such as towels, bath mats and blinds. Plain finishes on the walls are more yang, which is helpful here, but irregular patterns support water energy and would be enhancing. Employ them in moisture-resistant paint finishes, rather than fabrics or wallpaper. More yang materials (see above) are also beneficial. Colour and pattern can also be used to mitigate the effects of unfavourable bathroom locations. See pages 110 for specific solutions.

THE TOILET

Ideally, the toilet should be as inconspicuous as possible. To minimize its draining and flushing effect on the chi energy of the rest of the home, position it well away from the bathroom door. If the bathroom is large enough, site it so that it cannot be seen from the door, and make sure it is not reflected in any mirrors. Ideally, place the toilet in the east or south-east of the room, concealed behind a half wall, screen or curtain. Keep the toilet lid closed as much as possible, but especially while it is being flushed. Keep the bathroom door closed, especially if it is an en suite bathroom.

Leaking pipes and dripping taps or showerheads will exacerbate the draining effect of the bathroom generally and lead to dampness and stagnating chi. Blocked toilets are also counter-productive to a favourable flow of chi energy, so keep all plumbing installations in good repair. The draining effects will also be minimized if the bathroom is kept neat, clean and dry at all times.

THE BATHROOM FLOOR

The flow of chi energy through the room is strongly influenced by the flooring material, and different types have different effects.

Natural wooden flooring is neutral in its effect on the flow of chi energy, and helps to support tree energy, which is particularly advantageous in bathrooms in the east, south-east and south.

Marble, granite, glass and other hard, smooth, more yang surfaces speed up the flow of chi energy, especially if they are shiny and reflective, which creates a much more exciting, stimulating environment and one that helps avoid stagnation.

Stone and ceramic tiles have similar properties to marble, but if the floor is uneven they tend to scatter the energy. This can be an advantage in locations to the north, where there is a particularly high risk of energy stagnating throughout the entire room, and such floors are especially desirable if the bathroom has little or no exposure to natural light.

Synthetic materials used in flooring, including carpets and rugs and linoleum, or in accessories such as shower curtains, create their own charge of static electricity, which has a negative influence on the flow of energy and should be avoided as much as possible.

Curtains, blinds, carpets, rugs or mats made of natural fibres such as wool, seagrass, coir, rush, linen or cotton will tend to slow the movement of chi energy and make the room more comfortable and relaxing. But excessive use of any type of soft fabric can lead to stagnation and should be avoided especially in small or dark bathrooms. Fitted carpets, for example, are not generally appropriate for bathrooms.

FENG SHUI IN PRACTICE

Improving a north-west location

In my home the bathroom is in the north-west of the apartment – not a beneficial location. One compensating feature is a large skylight which allows us to keep the window slightly open and brings in morning sunshine. Also, the ceiling is high, the bathroom relatively spacious and its surfaces are hard and shiny. We placed three large plants with pointed leaves there, along with a red vase and flowers. The result is that even on the wettest winter day there is no lingering dampness. More importantly I have not felt the stagnation common in other bathrooms in the west, north-west or north.

solutions for bathrooms in fixed positions

Counteract the detrimental effect of unfavourable locations by harmonizing the bathroom's water chi energy with Five-Element chi energy in the relevant location. Eight Directions colours (see page 124) are also helpful. Determine the direction of the bathroom, then consult the chart below.

DIRECTION	EFFECTS	SOLUTION
NORTH unfavourable	The bathroom's water energy added to that of the north is overwhelming. The chi energy here is quiet and still, risking stagnation, which can deplete your vitality and make you too introverted.	Grow tall plants to introduce tree energy, thus draining water energy. They bring their own chi energy and vitality, absorb humidity and produce fresh oxygen.
NORTH-EAST unfavourable	This is the least desirable location because the soil energy here is destructive to water energy, stirring up the chi energy in a location already prone to quick changes, and leading to unpredictable changes in your life and possibly to eventual ill-health.	Introduce metal energy to help soil energy harmonize with water energy. Place sea salt in a white china bowl in the north-east of the room, or heavy iron sculptures or a red flower in a round iron pot.
EAST favourable	This is generally favourable because water chi energy is in harmony with tree chi energy here. However, the downward movement of a toilet being flushed and bath water being drained is contrary to a tree's upward movement.	Increase the upward tree energy by growing tall plants in the bathroom. Wooden flooring and fittings will also help. Using bright green in the towels and mats will also accentuate the tree energy of the east.
SOUTH-EAST favourable	Generally favourable, the effects are similar to those of a bathroom in the east, where water draining away may limit the upward tree movement.	Increase the upward tree energy by growing tall plants in the bathroom. Wooden flooring and fittings will also help.
SOUTH unfavourable	Water chi energy destroys fire chi energy here. This can lead to lack of passion, fewer opportunities to achieve recognition, and vulnerability to law suits.	Harmonize water and fire by boosting tree energy: grow tall plants and have wooden accessories and floor covering.
SOUTH-WEST unfavourable	The chi energy here is changeable and unstable, and the soil energy of the south-west is destructive to water chi energy. If unchecked this can lead eventually to ill-health.	To harmonize soil and water, boost metal energy by placing a small bowl of sea salt in the bathroom along with an iron pot or statue and something white, silver or gold.
WEST unfavourable	The metal chi energy here is drained by water energy, which could result in a draining effect on your income.	Boost metal chi energy by growing red-flowering plants. Alternatively, have red fresh flowers, or iron pots or statues.
NORTH-WEST unfavourable	Water energy drains metal chi energy, which could make you disorganized, disorientated and feel out of control of your life.	Build up metal chi energy by growing white-flowering plants, or have fresh white flowers in the room, or round silvery pots and metallic sculptures.

the home office

Working from home has many advantages. Not only are you able to set the pace of what you do and the way you do it, but you also have a greater measure of control over your working environment. You can choose where you sit, the kind of lighting that suits you, the shape of your desk and so on. This gives you the opportunity to design your office to enhance your productivity and effectiveness, so that you can achieve the success you are seeking. Everything in the room should be working for you, not against you.

Many people use a bedroom as a workroom, but according to Feng Shui principles it is difficult to create an environment that is equally appropriate for both sleeping and working since their needs are conflicting. It is better, therefore, to use either a spare room exclusively as an office or to locate your workplace in part of the living room.

One of the challenges with a modern home office, studio or workroom is to balance electrical radiation from the various pieces of electronic equipment with more natural chi energy. The positioning of your desk and chair in relation to computers, printers, telephones, fax machines and copiers, as well as their direction in the room are vitally important (see pages 113 and 116).

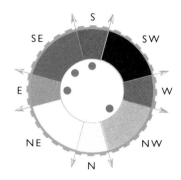

Recommended directions for a home office
East, south-east, south and north-west of the centre of your home.

FAVOURABLE LOCATIONS

Ideal positions for a home office are east, south-east, south and north-west of the centre of your home. Each has particular advantages which could be helpful, depending on the type of business you are engaged in, or the stage of your career.

The east has the chi energy to help you become busier, more active, more focussed and better able to put your good ideas into practice. This is the best position if you are starting a new business or embarking on a new career. The chi energy in the south-east is similar but gentler, which is more helpful for communication and the harmonious development and growth of your business.

The fiery chi energy in the south will help you attract attention for your business, and is more likely to lead to widespread acclaim and recognition for your work. If success is related to you being in the public eye, this is the place for your office.

The north-west is ideal for leadership, organization and for inspiring and maintaining the respect of others – qualities that would be helpful if you are working with, or perhaps directing, a team of people.

EAST AND SOUTH-EAST
Vertical stripes support the helpful forward-looking chi energy here; and blue and green are also supportive colours.

SOUTH *Purple maintains the fire chi energy here which will help you achieve success and greater public recognition for your work.*

NORTH-WEST *The metal energy conducive to organization here is enhanced by soil energy, so greys and whites with touches of yellow would be helpful.*

CHOOSING FURNISHINGS

The ideal atmosphere in an office is busy and stimulating, but not stressful. It should be a place you are happy to work in for long periods at a time, so choose furnishings that tend to be more yang, but balance them with restful more yin elements.

FURNITURE   The desk is the most important item (see opposite). The desk chair should also keep you alert while working, but not strain you physically or mentally. Much office furniture – filing cabinets, shelving systems – has sharp corners. Where it is impossible to find rounded alternatives, soften the edges with plants.

LIGHTING   Natural light is more beneficial than artifical lighting so, if possible, choose a room with one or more large windows. Avoid fluorescent lighting.

PLANTS   Plenty of leafy plants in the room balance electrical radiation. A peace lily is particularly helpful in this respect (see page 132).

ELECTRICAL EQUIPMENT Choose this carefully to mitigate negative effects of electrical radiation. An LCD computer screen, such as those on laptops, is preferable to a cathode ray tube monitor.

STORAGE   Work generates a great deal of paraphernalia – papers, files, books and so on. Have plenty of storage so that you can keep papers neat and well-organized, and avoid the stagnating chi associated with clutter. Avoid open bookshelves; cupboards are preferable.

USING COLOUR AND PATTERN

Check the direction of your office from the centre of your home. Aim to main the chi energy of favourable directions, adding enhancing or calming touches. Use paler yin shades and more subtle patterns to reduce the stress in an over-active working environment. Where the chi energy is too quiet and unstimulating for productive work, use brighter, stronger colours.

In the east the chi energy is busy and active; vertical stripes in bright and dark greens would maintain this helpful ambience. The gentler south-east could take enhancing colours; match blues or greens with cream and off-white on more yang plain walls. The chi energy in the hotter south will be maintained with middle shades of purple; soften it slightly with black and white touches. The north-west of your home is a more serious environment and is particularly appropriate to a more formal businesslike working atmosphere; try grey, white and maroon with touches of yellow. Check patterns are also suitable here, because they add soil energy which supports the metal energy of the north-west.

THE DESK

Your desk and its accessories (see page 114–5) both influence how productively you work. A large desk helps you to feel dignified and powerful. It also conveys the impression that you have room to expand. A small cramped desk can make you feel constrained, and that you have nowhere further to go.

A round or oval desk is usually preferable to a square or rectangular one. It is more relaxing to work at for long periods of time, and avoids the risk of cutting chi from sharp corners.

A wooden desk promotes a natural flow of chi energy, making you feel more at ease in your room. More yin softwoods like pine give a relaxed casual feel; darker hardwoods like teak and mahogany add formality. Glass is a stimulating surface for a desk, but is not as suitable as wood for lengthy working sessions.

POSITIONING YOUR DESK AND CHAIR

Over the years I have experimented with the position of my desk. I now work in a study which is located in the east of my home, with the desk in the east of the room, and I sit at the desk in a chair facing east. Since making these changes, my business has increased steadily, to the extent that I now need to consider a further change to help me consolidate what I have achieved.

The ideal situation is to sit in a beneficial location, facing a helpful direction, looking into the room, and being able to see the doors and windows easily. The directions on page 116 are some of the most favourable, choose the one that suits you best. Avoid sitting next to electrical equipment, which can lead to reduced concentration, fatigue and ill-health. Try not to sit with your back to the main door to the office, or with the door to one side of you.

In some cases your own needs may not be the only consideration. If several people use the office and work as a team, arrange the chairs to enhance harmony between them. Generally, it is best to place the desks so that the people sitting at them face the centre of the room.

If your work involves having business meetings at home, arrange the chairs so that your visitors feel positive about working with you. If your office is large enough, set up a special area for meetings. The principles are similar to those for seating guests around a dinner table (page 92) or in a living room. Each direction has specific characteristics which promote certain qualities in the people sitting in those positions. You can use this knowledge to seat people appropriately, depending on their own personal and professional characteristics, and on what you are hoping to achieve from your meeting.

FENG SHUI IN PRACTICE

Curing a workaholic
The chairman of a successful company was worried about the effect of overwork on his health. I discovered that his office was in the east and he sat at his desk facing north-east. This had made him too active, ambitious and hard-working.

I advised him to relocate his office in the north-west of the building and to face south-east.

Subsequently he became better at delegating work. He was able to run his company, instead of letting it run him.

Storage
Offices and workrooms generate clutter, which is obstructive to clear thinking and a productive working environment. Have plenty of storage units and keep paraphernalia neatly tucked away when not in use.

the desk top

The chi energy of your working environment is affected not only by your desk itself (see page 113), but also by the way you arrange the tools of your trade on the top. Favourable positioning can make the difference between a productive, creative, inspiring atmosphere, which helps you achieve your goals, and one that is frustrating and demotivating.

To make your desktop work for you, first determine the directions on it: place it in your chosen location in the room, then find the centre, establish magnetic north and place a grid of the Eight Directions over it. Place objects in sectors where they harmonize with the chi energy of that direction.

The western part of the desk, for example, is associated with finances and income, so keep loose change, cheques paid to you, or something made of gold or silver in this part. The south relates to public recognition, so the southern part of your desk would be an ideal place for any awards you have received. The eastern part of your desk represents the future, and here you could put something that reminds you of your long-term goals or your most cherished dreams. The north-east reflects your basic motivation for working. Is it material gain, creative fulfilment or something else? Whatever the case, place something that reflects those aims in the north-east.

THE DESK

Make sure your desk is large enough for your needs. Rounded corners will reduce the risk of cutting chi and the pale wood has a neutral effect on the movement of chi energy. The overall result will be a productive but not stressful working environment.

NORTH-EAST: MOTIVATION *Put objects here that will encourage you to work harder. They could be material, such as a financial forecast or the prospect of making a good profit.*

NORTH: TRANQUILLITY *Plants, especially peace lilies can help minimize the disturbing effects of electrical radiation from office equipment. They also bring their own living energy into the working situation.*

NORTH-WEST: ORGANIZATION *Keep your diary, forward planner or organizer in this position.*

 N

EAST: FUTURE DREAMS *This is the place for a reminder of what you can achieve with hard work, such as the car you've always wanted.*

FACING EAST *Place your desk so that you face a favourable direction while you work. The chi energy of the east is very active and good for building up a career quickly.*

SOUTH-EAST: COMMUNICATION *This is the right position for the telephone, the fax if you have one, and your mail tray.*

SOUTH: PUBLIC RECOGNITION *Keep things such as awards, prizes or other public accolades here.*

SOUTH-WEST: FAMILY HARMONY *Photographs or other mementoes of your family are appropriate here.*

WEST: FINANCE *This is the place for cheque books, cashbox and anything else to do with money.*

DRAWERS *Clutter obstructs the harmonious flow of chi energy so keep papers and desk paraphernalia neatly organized in convenient drawers and filing cabinets.*

positioning the desk and chair

There are 64 possible positions for the desk and chair, each offering a different mix of chi energies. The positions described below are some of the most advantageous. The desk position aligns you with the underlying flow of chi in the room. But the direction you face while sitting at it has the greatest influence.

	Sitting **NORTH-WEST** facing south-east	This is the classic position for a chief executive or top manager. North-west enhances leadership, organization and responsibility as well as dignity and trustworthiness. Facing south-east is helpful for expansion, creativity and communication.
	Sitting **NORTH-EAST** facing east	The motivating chi energy of the north-east combines with the active chi energy of the east, which is useful for someone lacking drive, or looking for a new direction. It is particularly suitable for people dealing in real estate.
	Sitting **EAST** facing east	Here the chi energy of the east is even more intense, favouring quick starts and fast growth. This is excellent for anyone starting a career or business, particularly in the computer or electronics industry.
	Sitting **EAST** facing south-east	This is similar to sitting east facing east, but the atmosphere is less intense, bringing out qualities conducive to communication, creativity and harmonious development. People working in the media or travel business are likely to find this supportive.
	Sitting **EAST** facing south	This is active, busy and helpful for putting ideas into practice. It is also supportive of public recognition and promotion, so would suit someone in PR, sales or advertising. However, it is not a good position if you feel restless and find it difficult to concentrate.
	Sitting **SOUTH-EAST** facing east	This is similar to sitting east facing south-east, only the relative importance of the directions is reversed. The location of the desk determines the underlying chi energy present. But the direction you face has the greatest influence, so the east is dominant.
	Sitting **SOUTH-EAST** facing south	This combination of energies is ideal for people working in PR, marketing or any activity that involves communication. It is also good for lawyers. The chi energy here is very active, so is not advisable for someone who becomes easily stressed or excited.
	Sitting **WEST** facing east	In the west you are immersed in the chi energy relating to income, contentment and pleasure. Facing east helps you to become more ambitious, active and better able to put your ideas into practice. It is particularly helpful for people working in finance.

other rooms

The principles of Feng Shui can be applied to other spaces apart from the main rooms. These can be whole rooms or parts of rooms. Not everybody will have enough spare rooms to devote one to, for example, exercise. But the following guidelines will help you choose where to allocate a space for these specialized activities and how to arrange them.

UTILITY ROOM Large pieces of domestic equipment, such as washing-machines, driers and large freezers are often housed in such spaces. The considerations are the same as for bathrooms since there is the same risk of dampness and stagnation. More yang surfaces such as glazed ceramic tiles counteract humidity and mildew. Keep all surfaces clean and dry, and plumbing in good order. Plenty of fresh air and sunlight will help keep chi energy moving. The least desirable locations are north-east, north and south-west. The south-east would be helpful, but not at the expense of the kitchen, which takes priority here.

EXERCISE ROOM People often exercise in their bedrooms, but to feel strong and active you need a more yang environment. Yellow, red, purple, orange and bright green are stimulating. Metal furniture also helps. Keep the space as empty as possible. Ideal locations are north-east, east and south-east.

GAMES ROOM The competitive energy suitable for games is found in the north-east of your home. This is ideal for physical games such as table tennis and billiards, as well as mental games like chess.

STUDIO/STUDY/WORKSHOP The north-east also encourages the chi energy necessary for creative hobbies like pottery and metalwork. The south-west is better for more practical, methodical activities such as DIY. East and south-east are ideal for practical creative activity – the south-east especially favours music-making; the east working with metal. The north favours study and inner development – good for writing or composing music; the water energy here is also appropriate.

STORAGE The north-east is a difficult location for many other activities so is ideal for storing things. A boxroom or built-in cupboards would work well here. Organize storage well and clear it out once a year.

MEDITATION ROOM There are different styles of meditation and people have different needs while they meditate. For spiritual activities generally, it helps if the space is peaceful and more yin, as in the north of your home, Alternatively, the chi energy of the north-west is linked with the trigram of heaven, which can make you more intuitive and more in touch with spiritual matters.

The ideal workshop
For creative activity of a practical nature – craft work, carpentry, furniture-making – a room in the east or south-east of your home would be ideal. It will benefit from uplifting tree energy and from plenty of light and sunshine in the morning.

guidelines for choosing decor

The decor has a profound effect on the chi energy of a room. When devising decorating schemes you choose colours, patterns and materials, and each choice has a specific influence. To choose decor according to Feng Shui principles, you need to take account of the room's direction from the centre of your home and whether or not this is favourable for it function. You need also to assess your own needs and aspirations, what you are trying to achieve in your home and your life generally. The chart below outlines the procedure. The sections on each room (see pages 79–118) suggest beneficial solutions.

ROOM LOCATIONS
Find the location and direction of the room from the centre of your home.

HARMONIOUS CHARTS
Check the charts on pages 123, 127 and 130 for harmonious colours, patterns and shapes for the direction.

LOCATIONS FOR FUNCTIONS
Check in the individual room sections whether the room is in a favourable or unfavourable position for its function.

FAVOURABLE LOCATIONS
In these situations you want to maintain the chi energy and perhaps add calming or enhancing touches. Check the charts for these colours and patterns.

UNFAVOURABLE LOCATIONS
In these situations decide whether the chi energy needs calming or enhancing to make it more favourable. Check the charts for colours and patterns.

YOUR NEEDS AND ASPIRATIONS
Decide whether you need to make changes to your life, or whether there are any problems you are trying to solve. If so, what kind of changes will be needed?

YIN AND YANG
Depending on your needs and aspirations and the room's function, decide whether it requires more yin influences or more yang influences. An office might need to be more yang, a bedroom more yin.

MORE YIN
Choose pale shades, patterned surfaces, less defined shapes and softer, matt materials.

MORE YANG
Choose brighter shades, plain surfaces, more defined shapes and harder, shinier materials.

NINE KI COLOURS
If the range of choice allows, choose colours that harmonize with your personal Nine Ki number (see page 37).

DESIGN ELEMENTS in FENG SHUI

Choose the objects you put in
your home carefully so that they
encourage helpful rather than
unhelpful chi energy. Colours,
shapes, materials, plants, water
and light, among other things,
all have implications which can
work for you or against you.

manipulating chi

Everything you put in your home influences the flow of chi energy. Colours, shapes and materials are all significant.

Some things have a powerful effect on the movement of chi energy, others a much weaker or neutral one. Even the empty spaces, or lack of them, between objects or in rooms and hallways can help smooth the path of chi through your home or obstruct it. The more active design elements include water, lights, mirrors, plants, fresh flowers, crystals, candles, sounds and sea salt. Things such as furniture, carpets, curtains and cupboards are less potent. Although relatively passive, your furniture sometimes defines where you will be in your home – your location and the direction you face. Its main function should be to enable you to spend most of your time in the most favourable positions. Doors and windows are important in that they affect the movement of chi energy into and out of your home, as well as through it. Staircases, similarly, channel chi energy in one direction or another.

Generally, it is the shapes, colours and materials of furnishings and decorative objects that affect the flow of chi energy. The shape of an object physically alters the way chi energy flows around it, and how chi energy flows into and out of it. The colour determines the light frequencies reflected into the room, which will influence its chi. Materials things are made of also convey very different kinds of chi energy.

feng shui guidelines for choosing furniture

The things you put in your home affect its chi energy, so it is important to choose furniture and other decorative objects that convey helpful chi, and to find the right places for them. Inevitably, you will have personal priorities, tastes and needs, and it is not always possible to get everything absolutely correct in Feng Shui terms. How best to compromise in specific cases is a matter of judgement.

ONE	TWO	THREE	FOUR
FIVE ELEMENTS AND EIGHT DIRECTIONS Look at the Five Elements chart (page 27) and the Eight Directions colour wheel (page 124) to check that the object will bring the type of chi energy you want in your life.	HARMONIOUS COLOURS, SHAPES AND MATERIAL Check the colours, shapes and materials charts on pages 123, 127 and 130) to ensure it will harmonize with its intended location in your home.	YIN AND YANG Consult the charts on pages 22–3 to decide whether it will make the chi energy in your home more active and yang or passive and yin.	POSITIONING Place the object where it will balance the chi energies: put more yang items in passive areas, more yin ones in active areas.

feng shui in practice

Whether you are trying to find the right place for a particular object, or the right object for a special place, Feng Shui principles can help you to make a successful choice. These examples show how the general guidelines (page 120) might work in practice with four typical problems to solve.

Placing a large plant

You want to find the best location for a yucca. The plant is tall with long tapering upward-pointing leaves. It is more yang and ideal for stimulating chi energy.

Solutions Because of the pointed leaves it will need plenty of space and should not be too close to seating or sleeping areas (to avoid cutting chi). A corner of a room where the chi energy might stagnate would be appropriate. The radiating shape represents fire chi energy. Green adds an element of tree energy, however the fiery appearance tends to override the colour in this case. Therefore the yucca would be harmonious in a corner in the north-east, east, south-east, south or south-west of your home.

Choosing a living room sofa

You have decided to place a sofa in the west of your living room and you want one that will increase that area's romantic chi energy.

Solutions The shape of the west is round, the colour red and the material metal. A sofa that has rounded arms, a round back and metal feet or castors will increase the chi energy of the west. Red will also increase it. Complementary colours here are white, yellow, black and grey. As red is a strong colour it need only be part of a pattern on the upholstery or on some or all of the cushions.

Finding an ideal bed

You need to buy a suitable bed to place in the south-east of your home so that the top of your head points east. The natural chi energy here is tree energy.

Solutions Materials, colours and shapes harmonious with the south-east are glass and wood; cream, green, blue and purple; irregular, tall and pointed. So the ideal bed would be raised off the ground (tall), with a natural wooden frame, and either painted in an appropriate colour or made up with cream, green, blue or purple bed linen.

Positioning a lamp

You have seen a free-standing lamp on a tall, thin, black metal frame, which you would like to buy, and you are wondering where to put it. Light itself is active and yang, and represents fire chi energy. The tall thin shape produces tree chi energy, the material metal chi energy and the colour soil energy. The most active ingredient is yang fire chi energy.

Solutions The ideal location for the lamp would be a dark corner where the chi energy is more passive. In the north-east, east, south-east, south or south-west sector of your home or room, the light will harmonize with Five-Element chi energy. So a dark corner in any of those locations would be a suitable place for it – but especially in the north-east and south-west where soil and metal energies would be in harmony.

using colour

The meanings of colour
In Feng Shui colours have various important associations which determine their effects. Off-white, for example, is more yin and is linked with the chi energy of the north; bright green is more yang than off-white but more yin than red; its links are with tree energy, and with the chi energy of the east; red is the most yang colour in this group, and is linked with fire energy, and with the chi energy of the west. On top of this colours have varying cultural symbolic meanings (red may mean romance or wealth, for example), and often specific personal associations for individuals. All these nuances can affect your choice of colour for particular purposes.

Colours influence the light frequencies present in your home and can change the chi energy there, whether they are used to paint walls, woodwork and furniture, or in soft furnishings such as curtains and upholstery, or in decorative objects. Even small amounts of a strong colour can have an effect. Colours can be related to yin and yang, the Five Elements and the Eight Directions (see pages 20, 26 and 31). Many Feng Shui practitioners use the Five Element colours, but I have found their relationship with the Eight Directions to be the most significant. Together with the centre, this gives you a palette of nine basic colours.

The outer ring of the colour wheel (page 124) shows the colours associated with the Eight Directions. These are the most harmonious colours for each direction. They maintain chi energy, which is a desirable aim if the chi energy there is favourable. Other colours can be used to enhance or calm chi energy in a particular direction. The chart opposite summarizes these relationships.

CHOOSING COLOURS

Colours can be used in two ways: as background colours over large areas and as accent colours in small areas. Background colours tend to be softer, paler shades, though this does not have to be the case, and accent colours tend to be stronger and more vivid, though again not necessarily. In Feng Shui terms, both uses can be effective if they are the right colours. The stronger the colour, the less you need for it to be effective. A small red cushion on a chair to the west of the centre of the room will be enough to enhance the chi energy associated with romance, contentment and income. To have the same effect, a soft pink would need to be used over a larger area such as a wall, large sofa or carpet.

The colours specified in the harmonious colours chart and shown in the colour wheel (page 124) represent a range of colours rather than a single hue. Different shades and tones of these same colours share their harmonious qualities but carry a variety of nuances. Brighter shades, for example, are more yang than paler shades (see also the colour swatches on page 125). Personal preference also has a part to play; if a colour has unpleasant associations for you, it would not be wise to use it whatever the charts advise. So when choosing actual colours for a specific function, do not interpret the charts too rigidly. See Chapter 3 and, in particular, the chart on page 118, for more specific guidance on choosing decor for particular rooms.

harmonious colours

Find the direction of the room you want to decorate, or of the furniture you are planning to buy, then check the Eight Directions chart to decide whether to enhance, maintain or calm its chi energy. When you have made your assessment the chart below will help you choose a suitable scheme. The colours in bold type are the most important. Yellow, the colour of the centre, is harmonious in any direction.

DIRECTION	ENHANCE	MAINTAIN	CALM
NORTH	red to pink / white to grey	**off-white to cream**	pale green / dark green to blue
NORTH-EAST	purple	brilliant white / **yellow to brown** / black	red to pink / white to grey
EAST	off-white to cream	**bright green** / dark green to blue	pale purple
SOUTH-EAST	off-white to cream	**dark green to blue** / bright green	pale purple
SOUTH	bright green / dark green to blue	**purple**	brilliant white / pale yellow to brown / black
SOUTH-WEST	purple	**black** / yellow to brown / brilliant white	red to pink / white to grey
WEST	brilliant white / yellow to brown / black	**red to pink** / white to grey	off-white to cream
NORTH-WEST	brilliant white / yellow to brown / black	**white to grey** / red to pink	off-white to cream

colour wheel

In the Compass School of Feng Shui each of the Eight Directions (pages 30–3) and its characteristic chi energy is associated with a particular colour, shown on the outer section of the wheel below. Using that colour in that direction in furnishings or decor will maintain the chi energy there. The inside ring shows the colours associated with the Five Elements (pages 24–9) which are favoured by several other schools of Feng Shui, and can be used as alternatives to Eight Directions colours.

Different shades of the colours can be used to produce subtle changes in the chi energy of an area. The swatches opposite show a variety of accent and background colours and their potential effects.

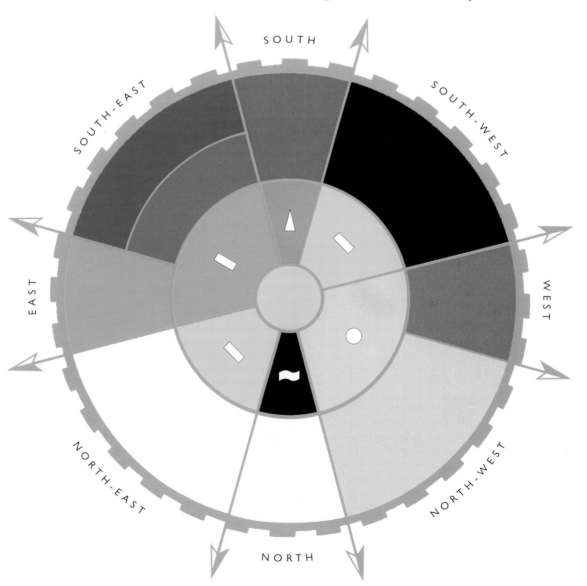

ACCENT COLOURS

Emerald green
This rich dark green best represents the tree energy of the south-east but with warmer yellowy tones, giving a lively excitement that is also settled and comforting.

Turquoise
Closest to tree chi energy of the south-east, this blue-green is more yin and creates a relaxing atmosphere but is still vibrant and uplifting.

Deep blue
Linked with the tree energy of the south-east, this strong blue would suit a sunny room. It helps to create a harmonious atmosphere.

Violet
Very close to fire chi energy of the south, this hot fiery purple will bring passion to a room. Good for sociability.

Peach pink
The colour of sunset, and closest to western metal energy, this enhances playfulness and romance – the right ambience for evening dining.

Orange
This hot sunny colour mixing red and yellow is closest to the metal and soil chi energies of the west and centre. Helps create a bright atmosphere in dark areas.

Chocolate
A deep rusty colour close to the metal and soil chi energies of the west and south-west, this enhances stability. Good in bright sunny rooms.

Mid grey
Closest to the metal energy of the north-west, this enhances feelings of dignity and authority and creates a more formal atmosphere.

BACKGROUND COLOURS

Citron
A sunny colour but with a lightly sharp edge, this is close to the soil energy of the centre. It evokes envigorating freshness coupled with warmth.

Lime green
Closest to eastern tree energy, this vibrant pastel symbolizes new growth and produces a bright optimistic atmosphere. Good for young people.

Eau de nil
Closest to the tree chi energy of the south-east, this mix of watery blue and green is yin and peaceful. It promotes creativity and relaxation.

Powder blue
This soft pastel blue creates a more yin gentler flow of the normally uplifting tree energy. It would be very soothing in bathrooms and kitchens.

Lavender
Close to the fire chi energy of the south though too pale to evoke fire or passion, this produces a more yin, mildly stimulating atmosphere, and is good for socializing.

Sugar pink
Closest to the metal energy of the west, pink is traditionally associated with the youngest daughter and enhances a youthful, playful atmosphere.

Pale apricot
A gentle warm colour which is closest to the soil energy of the centre but with a hint of western metal energy. Good for bedrooms.

Biscuit
A quiet light brown shade which enhances feelings of stability and security, this is closest to the soil energy of the centre.

using pattern

Patterned wallpaper, carpets, curtain and soft furnishings influence the nature and movement of chi energy in each room. The effect of different patterns is determined by the association of the shapes in them with yin and yang and the Five Elements (see pages 22 and 26). Similarly, the shapes in paintings, sculptures and other decorative objects will also have an influence (see page 147). If the pattern or shape is combined with its associated colour – for example, pointed patterns in purple, or circular patterns in red – the effects of both will be stronger.

PATTERNED WALLS

Walls are generally painted or papered. Plain painted walls are more yang than patterned walls. Irregular patterns produced by decorative paint effects such as sponging, colour-washing, rag-rolling and stippling are associated with Five-Element water energy, and create a more peaceful relaxing atmosphere. The use of creams, blues and greens would accentuate the calming effect.

Pattern is usually added to walls in the form of wallpaper, but stencilling, stamping and mural painting can do this too. Sharply defined, ordered and repeat patterns are more yang. Less defined, irregular or all-over mottled patterns are more yin. If patterns are pictorial (flowers, fruit, animals, country scenes) or have symbolic significance (stars, suns and moons), make sure the images have positive associations for you.

When choosing wall-coverings, check the room's direction from the centre of your home. Look for harmonious colours (see page 123) and check the chart opposite for harmonious patterns.

PATTERNED SOFT FURNISHINGS

The principles of choosing patterned fabric are the same as for choosing wallpaper. First check the direction of the curtains, soft furnishings or furniture from the centre of the room, and decide whether you want to maintain, enhance or calm the chi energy there. Consult the charts for harmonious colours, patterns or shapes. If your sofa is in the north of a room, for example, and you wish to enhance the chi energy there, circular or rounded shapes using a mixture of reds, pinks, white or greys would be appropriate for the covering fabric. If the sofa itself was rounded in shape, a plain pink cover would probably be enough. Take care not to overdo Feng Shui solutions until you have given yourself time to assess the effects stage by stage.

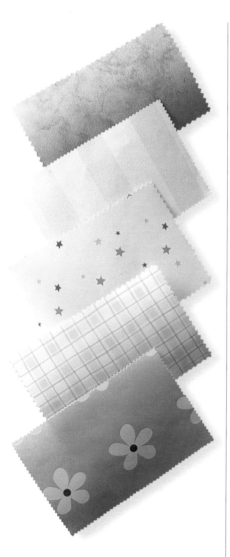

Influential patterns
The basic pattern groups can be linked with Five-Element chi energies: (from top to bottom) irregular patterns with water, vertical stripes with tree, stars with fire, checks with soil and rounded patterns with metal.

harmonious patterns and shapes

Find the direction of the room you want to decorate, or of the furniture you plan to buy, then check the Eight Directions chart (pages 32–3) to decide whether you want to enhance, maintain or calm the chi energy there. Then consult the chart below for suitable patterns or shapes. To place an object in a favourable location, find the relevant pattern on the chart and assess its effects in different locations.

DIRECTION	ENHANCE	MAINTAIN	CALM
NORTH	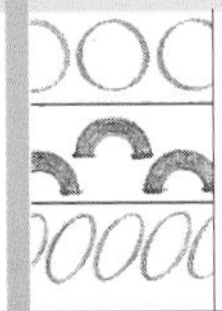 circles arches ovals	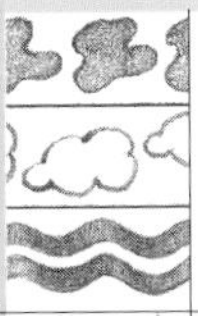 irregular clouds waves	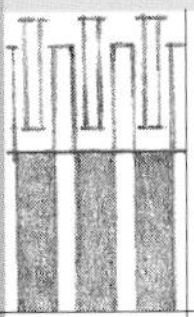 tall and thin vertical stripes
NORTH-EAST	 pointed stars zigzags	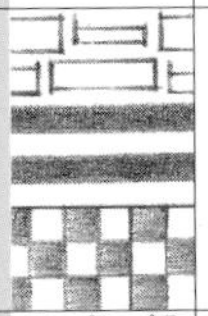 wide rectangles horizontal stripes checks	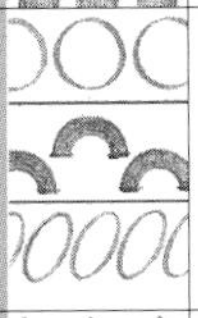 circles arches ovals
EAST	 irregular clouds waves	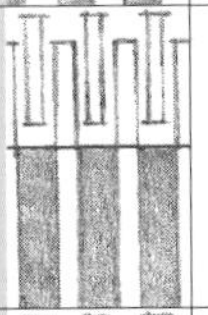 tall and thin vertical stripes	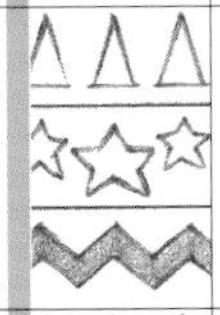 pointed stars zigzags
SOUTH-EAST	 irregular clouds waves	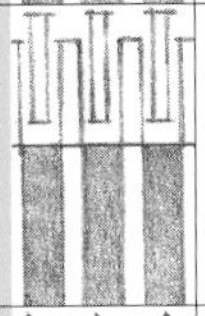 tall and thin vertical stripes	 pointed stars zigzags
SOUTH	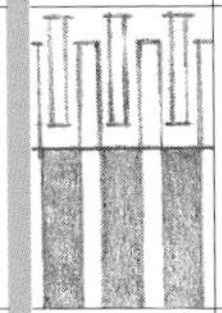 tall and thin vertical stripes	 pointed stars zigzags	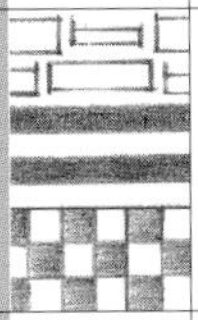 wide rectangles horizontal stripes checks
SOUTH-WEST	 pointed stars zigzags	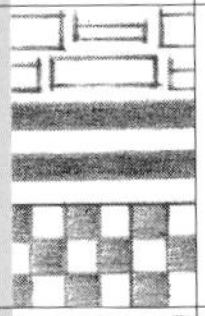 wide rectangles horizontal stripes checks	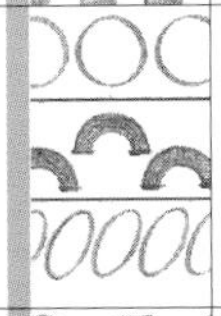 circles arches ovals
WEST	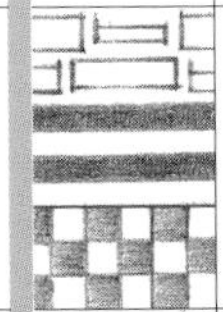 wide rectangles horizontal stripes checks	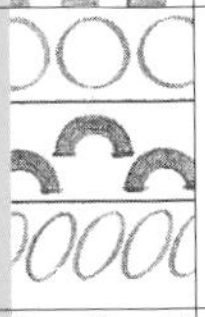 circles arches ovals	 irregular clouds waves
NORTH-WEST	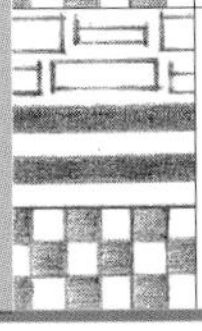 wide rectangles horizontal stripes checks	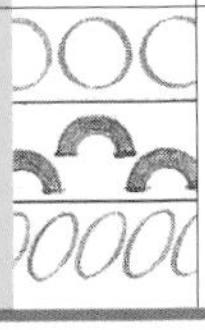 circles arches ovals	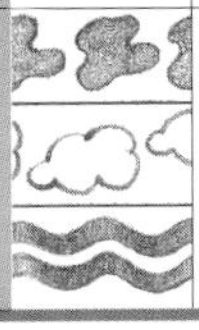 irregular clouds waves

using materials

The materials you use to decorate or furnish your home affect the nature of the chi energy in each part of it. The relationships between the Five-Element chi energy of the materials and that of the various locations in your home determine the effects, whether they help to maintain the chi energy of an area, enhance it or calm it. For example, things made of wood represent tree energy, and are therefore supportive of the Five-Element tree energy in the east and south-east of your home; in the south they will be enhancing because tree energy supports the fire energy of the south; in the north they will be calming because tree energy drains the water energy of the north. The chart on page 130 summarizes

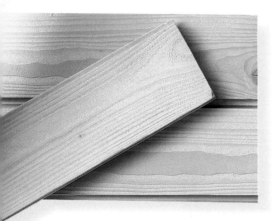

Wood
The effect of wood on chi energy is generally neutral, but smooth, polished hardwoods such as mahogany speed it up, and softer, rougher woods such as pine slow it down. Wood's great advantage is that it is easy to clean, and creates a light relaxing atmosphere without risking stagnation. It is most harmonious in the north, east, south-east and south, but can be used generally throughout the home.

Metal
Stainless steel, enamel, cast iron, chrome and other metals are all more yang and speed up the flow of chi energy. They are therefore particularly useful in areas prone to stagnation such as bathrooms, especially those in the north of a home.

Glass
Like metal, this also encourages chi energy to move faster, particularly when used in large single panes such as plate glass windows, doors, table tops or large glazed pictures.

Fabric
Curtains, wool carpets, rugs and soft furnishings slow the movement of chi energy, making a room more relaxing. Over-use of fabrics, however, can lead to stagnation. Ideally, fabrics should be made of natural fibres such as cotton, linen, wool or silk, but 80 per cent wool carpets are acceptable. Choose a natural underlay – felt is preferable to synthetic foam. Synthetics create their own static electricity, which has a negative influence.

Plant fibres
Matting made from rush, sisal, coir or sea-grass slows the flow of chi. It is the most yin type of flooring, being soft and highly textured. Its disadvantage is that it can be difficult to clean, so needs frequent vacuuming.

these relationships and will help you to choose appropriate materials for every part of your home.

In addition to the material itself, the nature of its surface influences the way chi energy moves through your home. Generally, hard, flat, shiny surfaces – such as on glazed tiles, glass, polished stone or hardwood – encourage chi energy to move more quickly, and create a more yang atmosphere. Soft, matt, textured surfaces – such as on unglazed tiles, rough stone, fabric, carpet, rush or coir – slow the flow of chi energy, which will create a more yin atmosphere. The larger the surface area involved, the more intense the effects will be.

When buying objects and furnishings for your home, or arranging decor, choose recommended materials where possible, with shiny surfaces for speeding up chi energy and matt surfaces for slowing it down. Avoid synthetics and plastics if practicable.

Ceramic and clay
Unglazed, matt ceramic or terracotta tiles are more yin and tend to slow the movement of chi energy, making for a mellower, calmer environment. Glazed shiny tiles with smooth reflective surfaces are more yang and have similar effects to marble and glass.

Plastics and synthetics
These materials have a blocking effect on chi energy, obstructing its free flow around the home, and should therefore be avoided.

Stone
Hard, smooth, polished stone such as granite or marble allows chi energy to move much faster, and creates a more exciting, but also more restless environment. It is unsuitable for bedrooms as fast-moving chi energy is not conducive to sound sleep. Softer stone surfaces, such as slate and limestone, have similar properties to marble, but rough and uneven surfaces scatter chi energy. This can be an advantage where you need to lessen the risk of stagnation. Rooms without daylight, such as bathrooms, cupboards and storerooms, may well benefit from stone floors.

Wicker, bamboo, rattan
Used mostly for furniture but occasionally for wall coverings, these materials have properties similar to other plant fibres and rough softwoods (see opposite).

harmonious materials

Find the direction of the room to be decorated and check the Eight Directions chart (pages 32–3) to decide whether you need to maintain, enhance or calm its chi energy. Then choose suitable materials from the chart below. To place an object you already have, check its material on the chart to assess the effects. Plastic carries fire energy, but is undesirable in Feng Shui terms, and should be avoided.

	ENHANCE	MAINTAIN	CALM
NORTH	metal harder stone	glass	wood wicker, bamboo, rattan plant fibres
NORTH-EAST	(plastic)	ceramic and clay softer stone fabric	metal harder stone
EAST	glass	wood wicker, bamboo, rattan plant fibres	(plastic)
SOUTH-EAST	glass	wood wicker, bamboo, rattan plant fibres	(plastic)
SOUTH	wood wicker, bamboo, rattan plant fibres	(plastic)	ceramic and clay softer stone fabric
SOUTH-WEST	(plastic)	ceramic and clay softer stone fabric	metal harder stone
WEST	ceramic and clay softer stone fabric	metal harder stone	glass
NORTH-WEST	ceramic and clay softer stone fabric	metal harder stone	glass

lighting

Light waves bring energy into a space and help activate the ambient chi energy. Artificial light is usually harsher than candlelight. Ideally, windows and skylights should be large enough to let in plenty of natural light during the day, so that artificial light is confined to evenings and dark days. To encourage more natural light into a home, open up more windows or build skylights in the roof. Pale colours on the walls and carefully placed mirrors can reflect sunlight into a room.

TYPES OF LIGHTING

INCANDESCENT LIGHT-BULBS used for general household lighting give a broad angle of uniform light. They increase the chi energy over a wide area in a relatively even manner.

SPOTLIGHTS allow you to focus the light in a particular place. This enables you to activate chi energy in specific areas like dark corners which are at risk of stagnation. Use them also to illuminate one area of a multi-purpose room for work while the rest of the room remains in natural or more subdued lighting.

UP-LIGHTERS encourage an upward flow of chi energy, which is particularly helpful if you have a low or sloping ceiling.

LOW-VOLTAGE LIGHTING produces a bright high-intensity light that is ideal for increasing the flow of chi energy through stagnant areas. It is easily recessed into ceilings and is also much used in free-standing lamps, which can be used for up- or down-lighting.

FLUORESCENT LIGHTING emits a different colour of light and also gives off more electrical radiation. In my view this can lead to headaches, loss of concentration and mental tiredness. The same applies to small energy-saving fluorescent bulbs.

COLOURED LIGHTING introduces more of a particular frequency of light. Check the direction of coloured lights from the centre of your home, and choose a harmonious colour from the chart on page 124.

DIFFUSING THE LIGHT

Direct light from bare light-bulbs is more yang and can be harsh. Lampshades, paper screens or plants placed in front of a light can diffuse it attractively. Reflected lighting also softens the harshness of direct light. Point the light on to a ceiling or wall instead of into the room. The lighter the surface colour the greater the reflection. This makes the more yang direct light softer and more yin.

Lampshades
Metal, glass or reflective shades create a less relaxing, more yang atmosphere; with fabric or paper shades it is softer and more yin.

electrical goods

MICROWAVE OVENS
▼

All microwaves leak some electrical radiation, and with age the oven's seal can deteriorate, but safe levels are being debated so the risks are still uncertain. In Feng Shui terms high intensity electrical radiation upsets the chi energy of the food itself. In my view people who regularly eat microwaved food can become disturbed and disorientated. There is no solution and microwave ovens should therefore be avoided.

***Counteracting the effects of
electrical radiation***
*Electrical appliances can have a
detrimental influence on chi energy,
but healthy indoor plants placed
nearby help to remedy this. Peace lilies
(Spathyphyllum wallisii) are
especially effective.*

Electrical appliances create their own field of electromagnetic radiation, which in Feng Shui terms intereferes with your own personal chi energy and may increase the long-term risk of serious illness. This is borne out by much current medical thinking. Studies have found that children living near power lines were twice as likely to develop cancer, which has led to concern about electromagnetic radiation from all domestic sources. Most electromagnetic fields diminish quickly so ensure there is as much distance as possible between you and the source. Transformers emit electrical radiation whenever the appliance is plugged in, so remove the plug or switch the appliance off at the socket. Leafy plants help mitigate the ill-effects (see left).

ELECTRIC COOKERS   The electromagnetic energy from these affects your own chi energy as well as that of the food you prepare, so gas, wood-burning or oil-fired stoves are preferable.

REFRIGERATORS Food stored in a refrigerator is immersed in a subtle field of electromagnetic radiation. Wherever possible keep food in a cool larder, outside during a cold season or in a cool cellar or basement.

TELEVISIONS   These generate an electrical field inside the cathode ray tube. Some of it leaks out. The intensity of this radiation reduces with distance so the further you sit from the television the better.

PERSONAL COMPUTERS   A computer monitor works in the same way as a television, and people sit much closer to a computer so the risks are higher. Hang a special screen in front of the monitor to reduce the intensity of the radiation. Better still, use a laptop with an LCD screen.

FAX MACHINES, PHOTOCOPIERS   Site them well away from seating or sleeping areas

ELECTRIC BLANKETS   The electrical radiation from these will be very close to you, so do not have them switched on while you are in bed.

HAIR DRIERS   The electrical radiation from these will be close to your brain. It is better to let your hair dry naturally.

ELECTRIC HEATERS   These emit fields of electrical radiation into the room. Gas central heating, gas fires or real fires are preferable.

MOBILE TELEPHONES   These emit microwave frequencies of electrical radiation close to your brain. This can heat up parts of your brain in a similar way to microwave ovens. It may be possible to reduce this by fitting a shroud to the aerial, or by using headphones and a microphone. It is better to use a traditional wired telephone.

WIRING Avoid routing wiring under your bed or near your pillows.

plants and flowers

Plants have a special position as decorative objects in the home because they are living things and generate their own particular flow of chi energy. Growing plenty of green healthy plants will create a fresher, more alive atmosphere. They help to compensate for the relatively dead materials often found in a modern home – electrical radiation from household appliances and static electricity from plastic and other synthetic materials. They also provide fresh air in the form of oxygen through their metabolic processes. Look after your plants well; wilting or dying foliage has a negative effect on chi energy.

Different plants have different effects, depending largely on their overall shape, the shape of their leaves and flowers, and their colour, which associate them with the Eight Directions, the Five Elements of chi energy and yin and yang.

Plants with pointed leaves are more yang and help to move chi energy more quickly. Plants with round floppy leaves are more yin and calm chi energy. Bushy plants help slow fast-moving chi energy and are effective in long corridors or near doors. Tall plants generate more tree chi energy, prickly plants and those with star-shaped pointed leaves encourage fire energy, low spreading plants produce soil energy, round plants or those with small round leaves metal energy, and trailing plants water energy. The green of the leaves also adds tree energy, but the colour of flowering plants adds more of the energy associated with that colour (see pages 136–7).

FLOWERS

Fresh flowers also add lively chi energy to your home, and they bring colour to a room in particularly vibrant way. The colour and to a lesser extent the shape of the flowers will influence the nature of chi energy in that part of the room. Flowers are most effective if they are healthy and well looked after. Wilting flowers have a negative effect on chi energy. Change the water daily and trim the flower stems diagonally to make them last longer. Remove dead flowerheads.

Although they are fashionable and popular in the West, dried flowers are less acceptable in Feng Shui terms since for some people they symbolize death and decay, but this is really a matter of taste and preference. Artificial flowers are recommended by Feng Shui practitioners if they are made of a suitable material such as silk or paper. Neither are as effective as living plants.

CONTAINERS
▼

Depending on their shape and material, the vases or jugs that hold the flowers can intensify their effects.

CURVED GLASS VASES add tranquil water chi energy, and are ideal in the north of a room or home.

TALL WOODEN CONTAINERS add the uplifting tree energy associated with building up your career, and would be ideal in the east or south-east. You may need to line them with a waterproof liner.

PYRAMID-SHAPED OR POINTED VASES increase the fire chi energy associated with fame, public recognition and passion. Purple would enhance this further. These are ideal in the south.

LOW CLAY TROUGHS OR BOWLS add more settled soil chi energy associated with family harmony, and are ideal in the south-west or north-east.

SPHERICAL METAL CONTAINERS enhance the metal chi energy linked with romance, contentment, style and income. Red and silver would intensify the effect. These are ideal in the west or north-west.

indoor plants

It is helpful to use a variety of plants in most areas of the home as their diverse qualities complement each other and provide a more balanced flow of chi energy wherever they are situated. But there are several specific situations in which they can be especially helpful (see opposite). Certain plants can have unfavourable effects in some positions. Spiky or thorny plants such as yuccas, palms or cacti should not be placed near seating or sleeping areas because of the risk of cutting chi. Take account also of the plants' relationship to yin and yang and the Five Elements when finding suitable places for them.

Ivy

YANG

DRACAENA (*Dracaena marginata*) The strong upward growth with sharp pointed leaves combines tree and fire chi energies. It is good for stimulating chi in a corner or under a sloping ceiling, but do not place it close to where you sit or sleep. Ideal in the east, south-east, south and south-west.

YIN

SPIDER PLANT (*Chlorophytum comosum*) The long, narrow, pointed leaves cascading downwards create a calming more yin atmosphere. Ideal in the north.

SWISS CHEESE PLANT

(*Monstera deliciosa*) Large floppy leaves create a more yin soothing chi energy. Ideal in any area that needs calming, especially south, south-west and north-east.

WATER

IVY (*Hedera helix*) The bushiness, upward growth and floppy leaves make ivy relatively well-balanced. But its clinging trailing habit means it generates water chi energy. It is useful in any area that lacks sunlight (such as an internal bathroom) because, unlike many plants, it will grow in shade. The ideal position for it is in the north.

Spider plant

Hyacinth

Poinsettia

Dracaena

TREE

HYACINTH (*Hyacinthus orientalis*)
Straight upward-growing plants add uplifting tree chi energy. From the pink, white, blue or cream flowers, choose one in harmony with its position. Especially harmonious in the east and south-east.

FIRE

AFRICAN VIOLET (*Saintpaulia*)
Purple star-shaped flowers make this plant strong in fire chi energy. It is helpful for attracting attention and getting public recognition for your efforts. The ideal positions are east, south-east, south, south-west and north-east.

PALM (*Phoenix roebelenii*) Upward-growing plants with spreading pointed leaves, palms add fire chi energy and create a more yang active atmosphere. They are ideal for corners. Avoid the north-east where the energy is already sharp and piercing. Ideal positions are east, south-east, south and south-west.

POINSETTIA (*Euphorbia pulcherrima*) The star-shaped leaf clusters can be red, pink, yellow or cream and the shape is linked with fire energy. Choose a colour to suit the location.

SOIL

CYCLAMEN (*Cyclamen persicum*)
This spreading plant adds soil chi energy. Choose a purple flowering one for more passion in your life, a red or pink one for romance and excitement, a white one for stability. The ideal positions are south, south-west, north-east, west and north-west.

EYELASH BEGONIA (*Begonia bowerae*) This white-flowering low spreading plant creates more yin soil chi energy, which is good for a settled, stable atmosphere. The ideal positions are in the south, south-west, north-east, west and north-west of your home.

METAL

MONEY PLANT (*Crassula ovata*)
Round thick leaves represent metal energy, which adds stability. The name is apt as metal chi energy helps finances. Ideal in the west, north-west and north.

PEACE LILY (*Spathiphyllum wallisii*)
This counteracts electrical radiation from computers (see page 132). White flowers add metal energy.

Cyclamen   *Money*

flowers

Flowers enhance the chi energy of particular directions depending on their colour and shape. If you feel the chi energy in part of a room or your home generally needs boosting, use the following: cream flowers in the north, white flowers in the north-east, tall greenery in the east, tall blue flowers or greenery in the south-east, star-shaped purple flowers in the south, low yellow flowers in the south-west and centre, round red flowers in the west and round white flowers in the north-west.

Clematis
Fill a bowl with the large purple star-shaped variety to boost fire energy and the chi linked with passion and social success.

Cornflower
The bright blue is helpful for travel and communication; the star shape for public recognition and an active social life. Place them in the south-east for going out and meeting people. Delphiniums would have a similar effect. Tall stems carry tree energy.

Pansy
Low yellow flowers carry soil energy. In the south-west they encourage contentment and family harmony. Primroses would also be appropriate here.

Fern
Tall green foliage plants such as ferns and grasses enhance tree energy and are therefore helpful in the east of a room to increase vitality and freshness.

Chrysanthemum
Place deep red chrysanthemums in the west to enhance romance and making money. Other possibilities are gerbera, dahlias and rosebuds.

Lily of the valley
The calm serenity of these white waxy blooms boosts the chi energy of the north-east. Place them in that part of a room to encourage calm, motivated resolve.

Pompon dahlia
These are almost spherical which supports metal energy, and the white variety placed in the north-west conveys the chi energy associated with dignity and wisdom.

Orchid
The flowing shapes and creamy colours of some orchids enhance the water chi energy of the north. Mixed with red or purple flowers here, they can help revive a dormant sex life.

Tulip
The bowl-shaped blooms
carry metal energy. Red in
the west adds romance, pink
in the west brings
pleasure, white brings
motivation in the north-
east, dignity in the north-
west, peace in the north.

Carnation
The round
shape of the
flowers and the
reds and pinks
enhance romance and
pleasure, whereas white
adds dignity
and serenity.

Mimosa
Flowers
composed of many
small yellow spheres
increase the chi energy
of the centre. Place them
in the centre of your
home to keep your life more
centred.

Iris
These come in many
colours especially
yellows, blues
and purples.
In spite of these
links with tree
energy and with the centre and
south, their delicate appearance
gives them a more yin quality.
Use them to introduce vitality
and passion, but gently.

Anemone
The shape is
linked with metal
energy and this with
strong colours helps keep
chi energy in one place.
Red anemones in a
western bathroom could
help prevent chi
draining away.

Lily
Despite
the tall
stems, the
flowers often point
downwards giving
them a more settling
influence. Use them to
quieten an over-active
part of your home.

Sunflower
The jagged flower
shape carries
fire chi energy,
but the colours
are closer to
soil energy.
They spread
out chi and
have a powerful
stabilizing influence.

Daisy
The
round white
flowers are
harmonious
in northern locations.
In the north they add
tranquillity, in the north-
west dignity, and in the
north-east motivation.

Rose
Tight round
rosebuds are linked
with metal energy,
but as they open this
changes to a more fiery
shape. Red roses will increase
the chi energy of romance
and style especially
if placed in
the west.

furniture

Chi energy moves more freely in open spaces, so keep some areas of your home empty so that it can circulate. Avoid over-furnishing or filling rooms with clutter, which will make it harder for chi to circulate and may lead to stagnation. This can be harmful to your health and may hinder you making changes in your life. In Feng Shui terms it is better to have a few things of high quality that make you feel good rather than lots of uninspiring bric-a-brac.

If there is clutter in your home, the likely effects will depend on where it is. A cluttered room in the north of your home, for example, could affect your health, vitality, sexual appetite, spirituality and your ability to find tranquillity.

It is particularly important to keep the centre of your home and of the rooms clear and uncluttered.

Where you place chairs, beds and desks determines where you and your family will spend most of your time. Position furniture so that you are in a favourable location and facing a beneficial direction (see pages 86, 98 and 116). The furniture's colour, shape and material, and in the case of antiques its history, can also affect the chi energy in a room.

CHOOSING FURNITURE

People often buy furniture that seems ideal in the store, but somehow does not feel right once they get it home. Feng Shui can help you choose furniture that is harmonious with its intended position. It helps you understand why certain items seem out of place, how to find the right furniture to fill difficult spaces, and how to find the best position for an existing piece of furniture. Check the relevant charts for harmonious colours, shapes and materials (pages 123, 127, 130).

Obviously, in some cases, practical considerations may override the requirements of Feng Shui and you need to compromise. Where materials are concerned, you can choose wood for any part of the home since its effect is largely neutral. If you were looking for a bedroom chair for the north-west of your home, for example, you would probably reject the harmonious materials (metal, stone) on practical grounds and choose wood, but a round upholstered shape covered in a circular-patterned fabric in grey and pink shades would also be an ideal choice.

New furniture contributes a fresh virgin atmosphere to a home whereas old furniture has absorbed chi energy from the past and has a more substantial feel. The kind of chi energy absorbed depends on the past use of the piece. A butcher's table will have absorbed a different kind of chi energy to a table used for displaying china. Find out the history of old pieces and check that it is compatible with your intentions for it. Most furniture will take in the chi energy of its new environment within a short time. Exercise particular caution with furniture that has been used for the slaughter of animals, or comes from funeral parlours, hospitals, or similar environments.

CUTTING CHI

Avoid positioning furniture so that sharp edges point towards you. This can direct swirling chi energy, known as cutting chi, towards you which causes your own chi energy to swirl and can lead to feelings of disorientation and eventually ill-health.

TYPES OF FURNITURE

BEDS Bedrooms with high ceilings can take high beds on legs, which enhances uplifting tree chi energy. Bedrooms with lower ceilings would be better served by a low beds or futons. These create a more settled, soil chi energy. (See also page 97.)

CHAIRS Rounded, soft, plump chairs are more yin and relaxing. Upright, straight-backed chairs are more yang and activating. Mix more yin and more yang chairs to create a balanced atmosphere. Use colours to create a contrast, for example a red yang cushion on a soft yin chair. The arrangement of chairs also has an effect (see pages 84–5).

TABLES The shape of a dining table has a strong influence on the area used for eating (see page 89). The shape should also complement the room. If you feel your dining room should be more relaxing, try a more yin oval-shaped table. Conversely if your eating area is part of your living room and undefined, you may prefer to use a more yang shape such as a round or square table. This will help keep the chi energy of the eating area in one place. Side tables and coffee tables should have rounded corners, especially if they are placed in seating areas, to avoid cutting chi. Yang materials such as glass on the table top will speed up the flow of chi energy and produce a more stimulating, wideawake atmosphere; yin materials such as light natural wood will have a more soothing effect.

DRAWERS The main consideration here is shape. Tall chests of drawers encourage a greater flow of upward tree chi energy whereas low wide chests of drawers bring out more settled soil chi energy. Round knobs, particularly if made of metal, enhance metal chi energy and give a chest a more solid feel.

DRESSING TABLES If this is in the bedroom it should have rounded corners to avoid cutting chi. Do not let the mirror face your bed during the night. Cover it with a cloth when you go to bed if necessary. An oval mirror matches the outline of your head and is better for feeling more relaxed while putting on make-up.

CUPBOARDS Built-in cupboards should be designed to avoid stagnation. Hard, smooth, shiny surfaces help to keep chi energy moving. Where possible they should square off a room. For instance, you might build the cupboards into an alcove to eliminate the corners of the alcove and avoid introducing more sharp corners into the room. This is particularly important in bedrooms. Place free-standing cupboards in alcoves, too, if possible, for the same reasons. Corner cupboards are particularly helpful as they cut off internal corners without adding any protruding corners. Keep cupboards clean and well-organized. Empty them at least once each season for a thorough clean-out.

Yang chairs
Ideal for a home office where you need to be alert and stimulated, yang chairs have hard shiny surfaces and are made of metal or dark polished hardwoods.

Yin chairs
Padded furniture with smooth curved outlines and soft fabric coverings is more yin, ideal for living rooms and bedrooms where you need to relax and wind down.

doors

Winding path
If the direction your front door faces is unfavourable to you, slow down the approaching chi energy with a winding path and plenty of bushy plants on either side. These will absorb unhelpful chi and dissipate its force before it reaches you.

Chi energy can flow through solid walls but it flows more easily through openings. Exterior doors affect the movement of chi energy into and out of a building; interior ones the way it moves throughout the home.

As you enter and leave a building through the main doorway you encourage a greater flow of chi energy. When your own personal chi energy field enters, it creates a current through the doorway similar to pushing water through an opening with your hands. Once you are inside your chi energy displaces some of the chi energy already there, causing further movement through the doorway. The same is true when you leave. The more people that pass through a doorway, the more active the flow of chi energy and the more influential the door becomes.

THE FRONT DOOR

The location of the front door defines the kind of chi energy entering your home. If the door is east from the centre, for example, your home will receive mainly the uplifting chi energy of the east. The more frequently the door is used, the more of this eastern chi energy will enter.

The direction the door faces also has an effect. A door east of the centre and facing east, for example, intensifies eastern chi energy. When there is a mix of locations and directions the location has the greatest influence. A door to the east of the centre but facing south-east lets in mainly the energy of the east, but it also catches some of sthe chi energy of the south-east The chart opposite shows the effects of different locations and how to remedy them if necessary.

OUTSIDE THE FRONT DOOR

To capitalize on a favourable location and direction, the front door should face the outside directly. If it is located to the north-west and faces north-west, for example, and you are involved in bringing up a family, enjoy feeling organized and have a leadership position in your career, your front door is in a supportive position, so a landscape that brings more chi energy to your door will be favourable.

If, however, you are in the same situation but your front door is located in and faces the north-east it is working against you. Here a curved drive with plenty of vegetation will slow and disperse the chi energy approaching the door. A long straight path speeds up and directs chi energy to your door. A tree, wall or building just outside the door will tend to block some chi energy moving to and from your home.

position of the front door

Check the direction of your front door from the centre of your home to find out what kind of chi energy is entering your home. If it is favourable, paint the door in a harmonious colour and choose harmonious materials for the door fittings. Some solutions for unfavourable locations are given below.

South
A highly active location – good for being noticed – but it can be over-stimulating, leading to arguments and possible separation.

Solution Bright green, dark green, blue and purple paint and wooden fittings are harmonious. Black will help calm chi energy, as will a low clay pot filled with charcoal placed inside the door.

South-east
Generally a favourable location – good for communication and harmonious progress.

Solution Dark green, blue or cream paintwork and wooden fittings are harmonious.

South-west
This exposes the home to slow settled chi energy, but is also along an axis in which the flow of energy is less stable.

Solution Black, rusty red or grey doors and shiny metal fittings are harmonious. A small bowl of sea salt would add stability.

East
A favourable location, especially for young people building up their careers.

Solution Bright green or cream paintwork and wooden fittings are harmonious.

West
The chi energy linked with pleasure, romance and income is brought in here, but it can also lead to laziness.

Solution Black, red and grey doors and shiny metal fittings are harmonious.

North-east
The house will be exposed to sharp, quick, piercing chi energy, which can lead to health problems.

Solution A high-gloss white door or shiny metal fittings will reflect north-east chi away from the house. A small bowl of sea salt just inside the door will help to subdue it.

North
This location is too quiet and isolated for an entrance.

Solution Boost the chi energy here with red paintwork, shiny metal fittings, lights and metal wind chimes.

North-west
This favours leadership, organization and feeling in control of your life.

Solution Black, red and grey doors and shiny metal fittings are harmonious.

Hall mirrors
Use mirrors in long narrow halls and winding corridors to slow down fast-moving chi and deflect it into other parts of the house, and to smooth the path of chi around bends or corners.

STEPS

If these are outside and immediately in front of your door, they can ease or obstruct the flow of chi energy into your home. Steps that go up to the door can slow its flow into your home and hasten its leaving, depending on the number of steps in relation to the size of the building, and on the surrounding landscape.

A large country mansion with big double doors and a long straight drive will not be significantly affected by steps leading up to it, nor will any house with a door to the east or south-east of the centre, where there is upward-moving tree chi energy. On the other hand, a cottage set in woodland with a narrow winding path to the door, would be greatly affected by lots of steps leading to it, especially if the door was small. It would be even worse if the door was to the south-west, west or north-west of the centre where the chi energy is more settled.

In basement flats steps often lead down to a front door, and chi energy can lie dormant in the stairwell. As the door is opened, stagnant chi energy enters. (See opposite for solutions.)

INSIDE THE FRONT DOOR

If stairs descend towards the main door from an upper storey, chi energy tends to move straight down the stairs and out of the door. As the chi energy leaves, it is harder for chi energy from outside to enter, which can lead to a deficiency inside the home. (See also page 146.)

If the front door opens into a long corridor, chi energy will speed up along the corridor as it enters the home, which can unsettle the chi energy there. Another potentially difficult situation arises if a second outside door is in view when the main door is opened. This can allow chi energy to enter through one door and leave through the other without circulating through your home. (See opposite for solutions.)

EXTERIOR DOORS

SIZE It is easier for chi energy to enter and leave large doors. They should be comfortably larger than the largest person in the household. If the main door is located in and faces a helpful direction, a large door is preferable. If the direction is unhelpful, a smaller door is preferable.
COLOUR Choose a colour that matches the location of the door (see page 141). If it is an unfavourable direction, a more reflective surface, such as a high gloss paint, will reduce the chi energy entering your home; it will also help deflect cutting chi.
MATERIALS Fully glazed or half-glazed doors let light through and also allow more chi energy into the home. They are particularly useful if you have a dark hall or corridor behind the door.

SOLUTIONS TO PROBLEMS WITH DOORS

There are a number of simple remedies you can use to ease problems relating to doors. First try one remedy and take a few weeks to assess the effects before employing additional ones.

Door fittings

Shiny brass fittings behave like mirrors and reflect chi energy away from your door. They can be useful if you have fast-moving chi energy directed at your home by a road, or cutting chi from a nearby building.. A door to a basement flat will also benefit from shiny door fittings. They will stimulate chi energy and counteract the risk of stagnation in the stairwell.

Plants

Bushes and trees can be planted outside the door to slow a flow of unhelpful chi energy towards your home. On the other hand, tall plants will help favourable chi move up stairs to a door. Indoor plants between the front door and staircase slow the movement of chi down the stairs towards the door. They also help to slow the flow of chi down a long corridor.

Wind chimes

Hanging chimes in the hallway or outside the front door can stimulate chi energy if it is stagnant or blocked by another building. (See also page 153.) A real metal door bell can have the same effect, but make sure it has a pleasant sound.

Mirrors

Where the front door is opposite a staircase, use a convex mirror to reflect some of the chi energy back into the house. Hang a large flat mirror on a wall at right angles to the front door to help you see 'round' the door as you open it. This encourages chi energy to flow smoothly past the door and helps you see into your home as you open the door from outside. If you have a long corridor or you can see the back door from your front door, use mirrors to deflect the fast-moving chi energy into other areas of your home, rather than straight out of the door. (See also pages 148—9.)

Lights

Where the front door faces a quiet direction, such as north, or is in a stairwell or dark cul de sac, an outside light helps to stimulate the flow of chi energy into the house.

INTERIOR DOORS

SIZE Larger doors induce a more active flow of chi energy into and out of a room and are best suited to living rooms. Smaller doors create a more intimate atmosphere and are better suited to bedrooms.

MATERIALS Solid natural wood is preferable to synthetic materials or bonded wood chips.

LOCATIONS The position of a door from the centre of a room influences the flow of chi. The effects are similar to those of external door locations (see page 141) but less intense; the remedies are the same.

POSITION Doors in a row encourage chi energy to move quickly in a straight line, destabilizing the flow of chi energy in the home generally.

OPENING AND CLOSING Hang doors so that they open into the body of a room, rather than into a side wall. This encourages chi energy to flow more easily into the room. It also allows the person entering to see the whole room immediately, and the people in the room to see who is entering. Keep doors open to help chi energy flow freely. To contain it in a particular room, keep the door closed. Keep bathroom and toilet doors closed. Keep your bedroom door closed while you sleep.

windows

Like doors, windows allow chi energy to flow easily into and out of your home, but as people do not move in and out to accentuate the flow, the influence of windows is not as strong. They let in light, however, and the direction the light comes from changes the chi energy in your home. Eastern sunlight is very different from western sunlight. To determine the chi energy entering through the windows, place the grid of the Eight Directions over your floor plan and check the their locations.

Ideally, the windows should expose your home to light from all directions (see also pages 55–6). Where this is not possible, consider installing skylights. These are a useful means of bringing in more light, especially in rooms with no windows.

Make sure all your windows are easy to open. Ideally, open them at least once a day throughout the year to allow fresh air and chi energy into your home, and clean them regularly. Replace cracked or broken panes promptly.

Finally, avoid sitting with your back to a window or sleeping near a window unless it is covered with thick curtains. Both these situations can be unsettling and make it difficult for you to relax or go to sleep.

Glass

Where the windows are large and the home exposed to plenty of sunlight stained glass is an attractive alternative. Use colours harmonious with the direction (see page 123). Clear glass allows the greatest range of light and chi energy to enter. Use this where natural light is lacking. Frosted glass, glass tiles and glass bricks are useful for privacy or in situations where it is not possible to use clear glass.

TYPES OF WINDOW

Chi energy enters and leaves a home more easily through large windows, but too many windows encourages too great a movement, making the home difficult to relax in. Too few or small windows risk chi energy slowing down and stagnating. Ideally, the number of windows should be balanced against their size, and the type of glass used in the window can help to counteract any disadvantages of size (see left). The window's shape is related to Five-Element chi energy and also has an effect.

Tall rectangular windows represent tree energy, producing an upward-moving atmosphere in the home. They are most harmonious in the east, south and south-east of the home.

Pointed or triangular windows represent fire energy but are rare in domestic buildings.

Wide rectangular or square windows create a more settled atmosphere, linked to soil energy and are best sited to the south, south-west, west, north-west or north-east.

Round windows are linked to metal energy. They create a more concentrated atmosphere and are most applicable to the south-west, west, north-west, north and north-east.

window treatments

The type of window covering eases or inhibits the entry of chi energy into a room. When it is exposed to favourable chi, you want to encourage entry; but in other situations (a bedroom at night or in a room facing a busy road) to discourage it. Curtains offer the most flexible covering. They tend to slow the flow of chi, but much depends on the type of curtains, whether they are light or heavy, full or filmy. Match the curtains to the situation. Clean curtains regularly to counteract dust and stagnant chi energy.

Curtains

In large rooms where chi energy can move freely you can use curtains. When drawn, full curtains create a quiet, cosy atmosphere, but in small rooms they entail a risk of stagnation. On small windows they may significantly reduce a room's exposure to sunlight, so choose blinds instead. Curtains in bedrooms help you sleep. If the bed is near a window or you sleep with your head towards one, draw heavy curtains over it at night to damp down the flow of chi through the glass.

Vertical blinds
These are associated with tree chi energy and are useful if you want to make the room seem taller.

Venetian blinds
Slatted blinds avoid stagnation but are less cosy. They allow in plenty of light so are useful for small windows. Wooden blinds have a neutral effect on chi; metal speeds it up, creating a harsh feel; plastics block the flow.

Roller blinds
Similar in their effects to slatted blinds, these create a slightly softer atmosphere because of the fabric. Use coloured or patterned fabric appropriate to the direction.

Shutters
More light is shut out by these than other coverings and, as they are relatively solid, their influence on the flow of chi is similar to that of walls. Some have openable louvred sections, making them more like slatted blinds.

s t a i r c a s e s

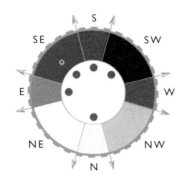

Favourable locations
The best locations for a staircase are north, east, south-east, south and south-west of the centre of your home.

Chi energy flows from one floor of a home to another mostly via the stairs. As people walk up and down the stairs they stir up chi energy and encourage it to move more quickly along the staircase, so stairs are usually a channel of fast-moving chi.

Steep stairs and long straight staircases encourage chi energy to speed up and move even faster. Twisting stairs slow the flow of chi and in most situations this is preferable. Spiral staircases spin chi energy, which can make the area where the stairs reach each floor disorientating. Stone and metal stairs encourage chi energy to move quickly across the surface; bare wooden stairs have a more neutral influence, and carpets, sea grass and rush matting all subdue the flow of chi energy. So a stone or cast iron spiral staircase would generally be regarded as doubly unfavourable in Feng Shui terms. If you have a spiral staircase in your home, the best advice would be to use soft surfaces.

LOCATIONS

The position of the staircase in relation to the centre of your home influences how chi energy moves up and down it. What is located at the top and bottom of the stairs is another consideration. Chi energy picks up speed as it moves along a staircase and, if there is an outside door at the bottom of the stairs, the chi energy tends to rush out of the house, leading to a deficiency inside (see also pages 142–3). Near the top or bottom of a staircase is not generally a favourable position for sleep, work or relaxation.

The east, south-east, south, south-west and north of your home are all suitable locations for a staircase. A staircase in the north-east will destabilize the flow of chi energy, whereas in the west and north-west the chi energy is more condensed – not ideal for the up and down movement on the stairs. A staircase running through the centre of a home tends to split it in two. This can, in effect, divide the family, leading to lack of closeness or even separation. Ideally, the staircase should be next to one of the outside walls.

To counteract the disturbing effects of unfavourable situations, place statues, bowls of sea salt or bushy plants at the top and bottom of the staircase. Something made of stone or metal is most effective in the west or north-west of your home, sea salt in the south-west or north-east, bushy plants in the north, east or south-east, and clay bowls filled with charcoal in the south.

decorative objects

The flow of chi energy in your home and garden is affected by any sculptures, works of art or decorative objects you place there. This includes paintings as well as three-dimensional items. The influence of an object depends largely on its shape and material. Images can also have an effect by their symbolic meaning, which influences your own flow of chi energy. A picture or sculpture of a couple in a loving embrace, for example, can encourage feelings of romance in you.

The influence of different shapes, colours and materials on chi energy is described on pages 122–30. By putting combinations of these properties together you can devise the ideal statue or sculpture for the effect you want (see right).

pages 122–30

HELPFUL STATUES

TO ENHANCE ROMANCE
Find a statue with a romantic theme, made of metal on a round base, with touches of red somewhere and place it in the west of your home or garden.

TO BOOST YOUR CAREER
A tall wooden statue with a touch of green or surrounded by plants, placed in the east of your home or garden would be ideal.

TO ENCOURAGE FAMILY HARMONY Choose a low clay or plaster statue in yellow, white or black, and place in the south-west of your home.

TO ADD PEACE AND TRANQUILLITY Place an irregularly shaped glass statue in the north of your home.

FOR FAME AND RECOGNITION Place a purple star or pyramid in the south of your home. It will be even more effective if it holds a candle.

Square boxes
These add metal energy. Use in the south-west to boost stability.

Clear glass
Place in the north to create a flowing atmosphere.

Shiny ceramics
Spherical shapes help concentrate energy in the west and north-west.

Clay birds
Low clay objects create a steady atmosphere. Use in the north-east.

Wooden animals
These add liveliness which is harmonious in the east and south-east

Metal boxes and frames
Use these to add solid metal energy in the north-west and west.

Stone figures
Romantic images boost the playful energy of the west.

mirrors

Convex mirrors
The curved convex surface of these mirrors will reflect chi energy in several directions and spread it out. They are particularly helpful for dispersing fast-moving or cutting chi, and on main staircases to reflect chi back into the house (see opposite).

Mirrors are very important in Feng Shui. They speed up and redirect the flow of chi energy. The hard, flat, shiny surfaces help chi energy to move more quickly, and their reflective quality deflects some of the chi in other directions. The effect is similar to the way they redirect light waves. Mirrors can therefore be used to direct chi energy and light to a part of your home where chi energy is stagnant. They can also reflect energy away from an area that has an excess of chi energy and deflect channels of fast-moving chi energy, unfavourable chi or cutting chi.

Mirrors are the most effective objects in these respects, but anything with a reflective surface can influence the flow of chi energy in a similar way. This includes shiny door knockers, knobs and handles, letter boxes, ornaments, glass-fronted pictures, polished metal pots and light fittings. Flat items, such as the glass in a framed picture, act like flat mirrors, shaped items, such as door knockers, like convex mirrors (see below). The more polished and reflective the surface, the stronger the effect on chi energy. They can be used like mirrors (see opposite), and are also useful in dark areas such as corners to keep chi energy moving.

To deflect cutting chi from a sharp corner or busy road away from your home (see pages 62-3), shiny reflective door fittings are more practical alternatives to mirrors.

MIRROR SHAPES

Two types of mirror are used in Feng Shui: flat mirrors and convex mirrors. Flat mirrors redirect chi energy in one direction whereas convex mirrors spread it out in many different directions. Convex mirrors are usually round, but flat mirrors come in many shapes including rectangular, square, round, oval, octagonal and irregular. Octagonal mirrors have special significance in Feng Shui as the eight sides are in harmony with the Eight Directions, but the other shapes can also be significant, and the material and colour of the mirror frame can also have a subtle influence on the surrounding chi.

Circular and oval mirrors are associated with metal chi energy, but whereas circles are more yang and help to contain chi, oval mirrors are more yin and therefore tend to disperse chi. Tall thin rectangular shapes encourage upward-moving tree chi energy. Low wide rectangles are associated with soil energy and create a more stable, settled atmosphere in a room. Like circles, squares are compact shapes and have the effect of containing chi energy.

using mirrors

Mirrors are used in many Feng Shui remedies. Positioned carefully, they can help chi energy to move more harmoniously through your home, and overcome the disadvantages of problem features such as long narrow corridors, small or L-shaped rooms and stairs opposite the front door.

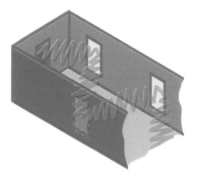

Corridors

Stagger mirrors on either side of a long corridor to move chi energy from side to side, slowing the flow. The corridor will also appear wider. In a dark, winding corridor position a convex mirror on the bend so that you see round it. If daylight is reflected in it so much the better; the mirror also helps chi flow round the bend.

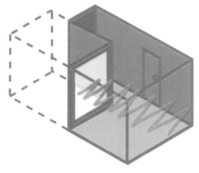

L-shaped rooms

Use large mirrors to give the impression that a room extends into an indentation. Hang them to reflect the space facing the mirror into the indentation. It will also encourage chi to flow across the room making the mirror wall seem further away. To be effective the mirror needs to be large, possibly covering the entire wall.

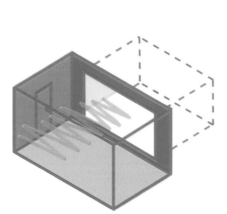

Small rooms

Large flat mirrors can make a narrow room appear wider. They also direct the chi energy across the room making it feel wider, too.

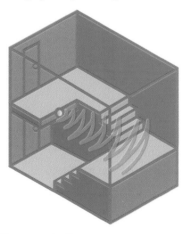

Entrance halls

Where stairs are positioned opposite the front door, place a convex mirror to reflect chi energy back into the house. Place a large flat mirror next to the front door so you see round the door as you open it.

GENERAL GUIDELINES

JOINS Hide joins between abutting mirrors with ribbons, strips of wood or plants. Joins distort reflections which disturbs the natural flow of chi and can make it difficult to relax. Avoid mirror tiles – fragmented reflections create chaotic chi.

SIZE Mirrors should be large enough for you to see your whole head easily or, in the case of long mirrors, your whole body. Hang them so that the reflection does not cut off the top of your head.

BEDROOMS Avoid having mirrors face you while you sleep. During sleep you expel unwanted thoughts and emotions through chi leaving your body. A mirror reflects some of this unfavourable chi back at you.

POSITION Do not hang mirrors opposite each other as the chi energy moves back and forth and cannot move on.

MIRRORS Avoid placing mirrors on window sills: this confuses the flow of chi through the window. Do not place mirrors opposite windows or doors as this reflects back the chi entering the room.

CARE Keep mirrors clean. Replace broken or cracked mirrors promptly.

water features

Swimming pool
Water is a powerful activator of chi energy, so a swimming pool can revitalize the chi of your home as long as it is in a favourable position – in the east or south-east. This pool is also a beneficial curved shape and is surrounded by healthy vegetation.

Water is one of the key solutions in Feng Shui as it has a special significance for the human body (see also pages 64–5). By adding a water feature either to your garden or inside your home you bring in fresh chi energy that can be highly beneficial for your health and destiny.

The water feature can take the form of a garden pond, fountain, swimming pool, bird bath, aquarium, indoor fountain or other indoor water feature. Even something as simple as a small bowl of fresh clean water can be effective. It is important that the water remains fresh and unpolluted. Place it either east or south-east from the centre of your home; no other locations are recommended.

PONDS AND FOUNTAINS

The most beneficial shape for a garden pond is a round or otherwise curved shape. To avoid stagnation fill the pond with fish, frogs, water plants, grasses and other living things. This will help maintain a good ecological balance in the pond and keep the water fresh and clean.

Moving water, such as a fountain in the middle of the pond, or an artificial waterfall, will help avoid stagnation. Fountains make the water more active and create a strong upward flow of chi energy. Lights in the fountain pointing upward will further intensify that flow. Fountains are particularly useful for protecting your home from fast-moving chi energy directed at you by a busy road and from cutting chi from the corner of another building. However, to be effective the fountain must be between your home and the road or the source of the cutting chi. (See also page 14).

If there is moving water, such as a stream, in your garden the direction of the flow should be towards not away from your front door. Water flowing away from you can drain your finances. Ideally, the water should flow towards your home in a series of gentle curves.

Waterfalls are another means of generating a more active flow of chi energy. Falling water has a more calming influence than the upward flow of a fountain.

Moving water in streams, waterfalls or fountains makes sounds which can also influence your personal chi energy. Water moving along the rocky bed of a stream flows easily around obstacles in its path. Similarly, the sound of running water makes chi energy move easily around obstacles in its path. If you are going through a rocky stage in your life, it can help you get through.

The sound of gently trickling water is more yin and soothing, whereas the loud crashing sound of a tumbling waterfall or tall strong fountain is more yang and stimulating. Completely still clean water with a calm smooth surface is the most yin.

SWIMMING POOLS

Site the pool in a favourable direction – east or south-east from the centre of your home. Swimming pool water usually has chemicals added to prevent bacteria and algae growth, so in a sense it is somewhat polluted and not ideal. The pool's shape should not incorporate sharp corners. Rectangles with rounded corners, or oval or irregular curved shapes would all be beneficial. Do not position the pool close to your home or close to a door.

An indoor pool should be in the east or south-east of your home. It must be well-ventilated and designed so that there is minimal risk of condensation or damp entering the rest of your home. Keep doors between the pool and the rest of the house closed.

INDOOR WATER FEATURES

An aquarium is a favourite means of bringing moving water indoors. Place the tank east or south-east from the centre of your home and if possible to the east or south-east from the centre of the room. Use pebbles and shells rather than plastic decoration. Appropriate living plants in the water will add their own chi energy and help keep the tank clean and the fish healthy.

Indoor fountains can vary from elaborate structures to a small rock with an integral pump that moves water to the top of the rock and allows it to trickle down again. As with aquariums, these should be located to the east or south-east of the centre of your home or the room.

If you do not have the space for a more elaborate water feature place a bowl of water to the east or south-east of your home. Refill it each day. Ideally, the bowl should be refilled from a tap in the east or south-east of the home before any other water is taken from it.

FISH

The fish you put into a pond or aquarium have an effect on chi energy; depending on their shape, colour and behaviour they can be more yin or more yang. Quick aggressive fish darting backwards and forwards will create a more yang dynamic flow of chi. Brightly coloured fish are also stimulating. Slow, peaceful fish, or fish with muted colours are more yin and promote a gentler more relaxing atmosphere.

FENG SHUI IN PRACTICE

Water cures

One of my clients was unhappy that since her divorce three years earlier she had not met anyone new.

I advised her to place a bowl of water on the window sill along the east-west axis of her home. She refilled it with fresh water each day when she got up. The water was in a place where the afternoon sun fell on it. Within a few months she had met three men who want to get to know her better.

Another self-employed client was experiencing difficulties in various aspects of his life including his business. On my advice he placed an aquarium with brightly coloured quick-moving fish in the east of his home. After a while he realised that his business had increased by 70 per cent. He began to feel more positive and confident about the future and better able to deal with problems.

151

other chi activators

Using crystals
Hung in a window, crystals can bring chi energy from outside into dark or stagnant areas of your home.

Certain small items can be used to activate chi in a variety of contexts and in a particularly powerful way. These include crystals, lighted candles, things that make beautiful sounds and sea salt.

CRYSTALS

As sunlight passes through a crystal it refracts into the colours of the rainbow. Beams of coloured light radiate in all directions, each colour carrying the intensity of that particular type of chi energy. Green carries the tree chi energy of the east, for example.

The commonest crystals are round multi-faceted ones. They have many flats machined on to the surface which increase their ability to refract light in many directions. They often come with an eyelet and cord for hanging. Irregularly shaped or jagged crystals can also be used but take care to avoid creating too much spiky chi. Place them near plants whose own yin chi energy will help smooth that of the crystal.

CANDLES

Candles bring fire chi energy to an area, which encourages more passion and expressiveness, and helps attract attention. If you gaze at a candle while meditating it can encourage the development of new ideas; use a solitary candle for this as it provides a single point of focus. If you are hoping to develop a more intimate relationship with someone, place a pair of candles close together. Tall candles are the most suitable shape since they represent tree energy which is supportive to fire.

The most favourable locations for candles are in the east, south-east, south, south-west, centre and north-east of your home, and of a particular room. You can keep the candle burning continuously, or while you are in the room, or when that direction is most active (see pages 30–3).

Candles are helpful where a home or room is lacking sunlight. Place several candles in the south of the room or in the corner. In dark damp rooms candles make the atmosphere drier and brighter.

The shape, material and colour of the candle holder will have a subtle influence on the surrounding chi energy. A tall, black, wrought iron holder, for example, is associated with tree, soil and metal chi energies, a tall, green, wooden holder has all the characteristics of tree chi energy, a flat white china holder soil chi energy.

White candles have the closest relationship to the flame of the candle and, in most situations, are preferable to coloured candles.

SOUNDS

Sound vibrates the air, which stimulates chi energy. Chanting and singing can achieve this in the human body. Wind chimes, bells and gongs, ticking clocks and the sound of running water are also helpful.

WIND CHIMES You can use wind chimes inside the home and in the garden. The tone is intended to purify and cleanse chi energy, so choose chimes carefully for the sweetness and clarity of their sound. Chimes are usually made of metal, wood or pottery, which enhance the elements of metal, tree and soil respectively. When you have decided where the chimes should be, check that direction from the centre of your home and choose an appropriate material (see page 130). To stimulate the chi energy near a door in the north of your home, for example, hang metal chimes so that they sound when the door is opened. To calm the chi energy of the south, pottery chimes are more suitable.

BELLS AND GONGS Traditionally, these have been used to clear chi energy in a part or all of the home. They can be rung by hand in areas that feel heavy or stagnant. A gong hung in a hallway near the centre of the home will sound throughout the house each time it is struck. Other ringing sounds have a similar effect. If the sound is generated by a metal bell rather than electronically, telephone and door bells can enhance the flow of chi energy. All these are stimulating and can help keep the chi energy clear and fresh.

CLOCKS The rhythmic tick of a grandfather clock creates a more yang, ordered chi energy, which could be useful if you need to get some order into your life. The regular chimes of the clock periodically clear chi energy and add another dimension to the ticking.

SEA SALT

Salt is the most yang of the foods we eat. It is found in blood in the form of sodium and thus has a direct influence on your personal chi energy. It also has the ability to draw moisture out of the atmosphere, and in Feng Shui terms its effect is to pull chi energy into it, which tends to have a purifying and stabilizing influence. This contracting inward-moving chi is associated with Five-Element metal energy, so you can use sea salt in situations where it will be in harmony with that. Place one or two tablespoons of salt in a low white china bowl. Place the bowl on the floor, or on a shelf or table if you have children or pets. Alternatively, tuck it out of sight behind a piece of furniture

Sea salt is most effective in the north-east and south-west of the house where the metal energy of the salt will help stabilize the naturally less stable flow of soil chi. This is especially useful if you have a door, stairs, bathroom, toilet or kitchen in these directions.

Making sounds
Whether they are loud or soft, sounds can stimulate or cleanse chi energy particularly in areas prone to stagnation, such as dark corners, corridors, hallways or under sloping roofs. Wind chimes, bells and clocks are all possibilities. To have positive rather than negative effects, sounds must be pleasing to the ear, so choose them carefully.

finding a new home

Moving to a new home is a major event in most people's lives. In Feng Shui terms it presents opportunities for revitalizing all aspects of your life, but it also entails powerful risks. In retrospect, moving home often turns out to have been a significant turning point in your career as well as your personal life. So choosing the right home is one of the most important decisions you can make.

Before making a decision, check that the potential of the new home is favourable to your aims and ambitions rather than unfavourable. Both the timing and direction of your move should be working for you rather than against you.

Once you have established one or more favourable directions, and you have identified potentially suitable homes, check the relevant

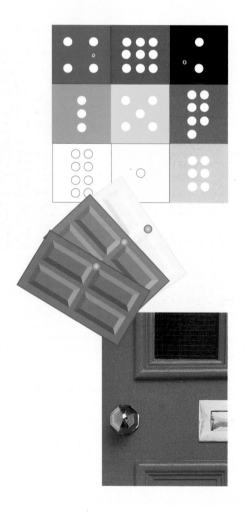

DIRECTION In which direction are you moving? Is it compatible with the Nine Ki year of your move? If not, consider another direction. *See page 40.*

PREVIOUS OCCUPANTS What happened to the previous occupants? Were they successful and happy in the home? If not, assess whether the chi of the home could be responsible. *See page 13.*

BUILDING MATERIALS What materials are used in the construction of the building? What effects are they likely to have? *See page 49.*

BUILDING SHAPE What is the shape of the house, and what are the likely effects of any extensions or indentations? *See page 51.*

OTHER BUILDINGS What kinds of buildings are located nearby? Are they likely to cause problems and, if so, how near are they? *See page 56.*

SUNLIGHT Which way does the building face? Is there good exposure to sunlight? If not, can this be corrected, for example, by opening up more windows? *See page 54.*

NEIGHBOURING BUILDING SHAPES What shapes are the neighbouring buildings? Are they compatible with the shape of your new home. *See page 56.*

SHADOWS Is the home overshadowed by nearby buildings? If so, from what directions? *See page 60.*

ROADS What is the home's position in relation to nearby roads? Are they likely to disrupt its chi energy? *See page 63.*

WATER Is there water nearby? If so, what kind of water is it, and what direction is it from the home? *See page 64.*

HILLS If the building is on a hill, where on the hill is it sited, and which way does it face? *See page 66.*

TREES Are there trees nearby? If so, are they healthy? What kind of trees are they? Are they located in helpful directions from the house? *See page 66.*

FRONT DOOR Is the position of the front door favourable? If not, can it be moved, or the situation remedied? *See page 140.*

features of the building's exterior, its architecture and the surrounding landscape (this applies whether you are looking at a house or apartment). The history of the home and its previous occupants are also important.

Finally, acquire a floor plan of the home and establish the directions of the main rooms. Use this to check key features of the home's interior, especially those which are difficult to relocate such as main doors, bathrooms and kitchens. It is unlikely that you will find the perfect home, one that complies with the principles of Feng Shui in all respects. More often you will need to compromise. Some problem features are more serious than others, and some are more easily remedied than others. Bear in mind also that the home must favour your own particular aims and aspirations and not some abstract ideal.

The following checklist of questions will help you to conduct your own Feng Shui assessment of the home, giving you an idea of the problems you can expect, and help you to take corrective action if necessary.

FRONT DOOR APPROACH Is the approach to the front door favourable? If not, can it be remedied? *See page 140.*

MAIN STAIRCASE Is the position of the main staircase favourable? If not can it be changed or remedied? *See page 146.*

LIVING ROOM FURNITURE Will it be possible to position living room chairs and sofas favourably? *See pages 84, 86.*

BEDROOMS Will it be possible to position your bedroom and bed and those of your children favourably? *See pages 93, 98, 99.*

HOME OFFICE AND DESK Will it be possible to position your office and your desk and desk chair favourably? *See pages 111, 116.*

KITCHEN Is the kitchen located in a favourable direction? If not, can it be moved? Are the sink and stove favourably sited in relation to each other? If not, can they be moved? *See page 103.*

BATHROOM What are the locations of the bathrooms, showers and toilets in relation to the centre of the house? If they are unfavourable can they be moved? *See page 107.*

BEFORE MOVING INTO A NEW HOME

To clear out any negative chi energy left there from past events or previous occupants, spring-clean your new home thoroughly before you move in. Ideally, redecorate throughout, replace all carpets and curtains and remove any soft furnishings left behind.

Cleaning will be most effective in spring and summer as, at those times of year, chi energy is more yang and upward. Choose a dry, sunny day to activate the old chi energy and enable it to leave your home more easily.

If your move has to take place in autumn or winter, have a second major clean, and if possible redecorate, as soon as spring comes.

INDEX

ACKNOWLEDGEMENTS

I would like to thank all those who have played their part in helping me to arrive at the place where I could write this book: all the Browns especially my mother Patsy, Dragana the love of my life, my children Christopher, Alexander, Nicholas and Michael, also Adam and Angela and their children; the Waxmans, especially Melanie and Denny, for getting me started; an enormous thank you to Boy George for all his help; my friends and clients Kim Andreolli, Adrienne Brown, Jasna Cacik, Enno and Dusica von Landmann, Michael Maloney, the Mosbachers, and my oldest friend Jeremy Parkin; my teachers and colleagues Michio and Aveline Kushi, Shizuko Yamamoto, Marc van Cauwenberghe, Saul Goodman, Patrick McCarty, Patrick Riley, William Spear, Bill Tara and Rik Vermuyten; all those I have worked with including Gina Lazenby and her staff, Ginie Lyras and her staff, Harriet and Paul McNeer and Krista and Reid Berman; a special thank you to all my clients who have given me the opportunity to put Feng Shui into practice; and everyone at Carroll and Brown, especially Amy Carroll, Denise Brown and Sandy Carr.

SIMON BROWN

about the author

SIMON BROWN began studying Oriental medicine in 1981 and qualified as a Shiatsu therapist and macrobiotic consultant. While learning these healing arts he became interested in Feng Shui. For seven years he was the director of London's Community Health Foundation, which ran a wide range of courses in Oriental therapies. He has since made Feng Shui his full-time career, giving private consultations and lecturing in the USA and Europe. His clients include celebrities such as Boy George, and large companies like The Body Shop and British Airways.

CARROLL & BROWN would also like to thank the following:

ILLUSTRATIONS D. Brown, Peter Campbell, Karen Cochrane

MODEL-MAKING Robert Bradshaw, painter and miniaturist

PICTURE RESEARCH Sandra Schneider

INDEX Madeline Weston

PHOTOGRAPHIC SOURCES Jean-Paul Bonhommet (EWA), pages 47, 76 (right), 117; Michael Dunne (EWA), 77 (left); EWA, 140, 144, 148; Brian Harrison (EWA), 6 (left), 8-9 (bottom left, bottom right), 67; Rodney Hyatt (EWA), 8-9 (top); Andrew Kolesnikow (EWA), 142; Tom Leighton (EWA), 8-9 (bottom right); Neil Lorimer (EWA), 7 (left), 76 (left), 150; Spike Powell, interior designer – Sethna & King (EWA), 69 ; Science Photo Library 13, 18 (bottom); Tony Stone Images, 49 (far left), 57 (second left) 64; Jerry Tubby (EWA), 77 (right); Zefa, 18 (top).

EWA = Elizabeth Whiting Associates

All books by Simon Brown use the compass style of Feng Shui.

Practical Feng Shui for Business (Ward Lock ISBN 0 7063 7768 0). Ideal for anyone who wants to apply Feng Shui to their career. This book explains how to be more successful at work. The book is full of colourful drawings and photographs to help you to implement Feng Shui in real life situations. It includes successful strategies for offices, shops and restaurants.

Practical Feng Shui Astrology (Ward Lock ISBN 0 7063 7825 3). Using the Nine Ki system this book shows you how to make and read your own chart. This can then be used to gain interesting insights into your relationships with lovers, friends and family. This book helps you to work out the best time to make important changes in your life and highlights th e most favourable times of year for you. The book is in full colour with quick reference charts that make it fun and easy to use.

The Principles of Feng Shui (Thorsons ISBN 0 7225 3347 0). A simple introduction that takes you through each stage in learning Feng Shui. The aim is to help you understand how Feng Shui works and then provides useful information to apply Feng Shui. Full of real life examples and useful tips. Includes a checklist for buying a new home and advice in finding a Feng Shui consultant. This is now also available as an audio cassette.

For information on Feng Shui consultations with Simon Brown contact:
PO Box 10453, London NW3 4WD, England.
Tel/Fax 00-44-171-431 9897.
e-mail 106025.3515@compuserve.com.

Visit his web site, including software for floor plans and Nine Ki information, on:
HTTP://ourworld.compuserve.com/homepages/simonbrown_fengshui